History

Been There All Along

Praise for *Been There All Along*

Marco Pardo, rehabilitation counselor and spiritual director:

Fr. Tracy O'Sullivan's *Been There All Along* is a brave and fiercely honest reflection on a lifelong desire and struggle to be an authentic man of faith. At times stunning and always refreshing are the remembrance of his struggles with his demons while discovering God's grace and mercy in those struggles. His disarming candor and fidelity to his vocations as priest, Carmelite, and disciple of Jesus are a challenge and invitation to us who read this work to be equally honest as we remain open to God's mercy and ever-present love.

Fr. Jack Stoeger, Director of the Cardinal Manning House of Prayer for Priests in Los Angeles:

As believers (whether we realize it or not) we "write" our gospel – the "good news" of how we have come to know and walk with Jesus – and how that ongoing relationship shapes and transforms our lives and, through us, the lives of others. Fr. Tracy's very honest story will assist those who read it to connect with their own experience of God's action and mercy in their lives! His living a Carmelite life and spirituality enables and challenges us to discover and live a spirituality that best engenders God's life in us. Especially as we mature, look back, and remember, we too will begin to realize that it is indeed true: God, who writes straight with crooked lines has "been there all along."

Fr. Joseph Chalmers, O. Carm., former Prior General of the Carmelites (1995-2007) and presently spiritual director at St. Luke's Institute:

Tracy O'Sullivan has lived an interesting life and has been involved in some of the major civil and ecclesiastical movements of the 20th century. He has seen the rise of the civil rights movement and the heady days of the Second Vatican Council with its call for the renewal of the liturgy.

In the midst of all these exciting events, Tracy was struggling with his own dependence on alcohol. He discovered a great strength in Carmelite spirituality. What gives his life meaning now and is the golden thread linking the many different aspects of his long life is that of contemplation, the openness to an intimate relationship with God.

Tracy O'Sullivan has the heart of a pastor and a great love for his Carmelite vocation. Both these aspects shine out from the pages of his autobiography, which will greatly reward the attentive reader.

Mark Mitchell, marriage and family therapist:

Tracy tells a story of a quarterback's struggle on the God Squad and how after being tackled, clipped, tripped, and confused, he hears the call of the Coach.....A great & inspiring read.

Fr. Donald Buggert, O. Carm., retired, professor of Systematic Theology at the Washington Theological Union:

This is the spiritual autobiography of a Carmelite friar and priest and his fifty-one year contemplative search for God, primarily in his work with and for those marginalized by the unjust and dehumanizing socio-economic system and structures of our American society. The life and struggles of "this dangerous little friar," at times a thorn in the side of both prelates and politicians, reveals that God is "always already there," hidden in the mix of the weeds and the wheat.

Fr. John Welch, O. Carm., former professor at the Washington Theological Union and prize winning author of books on Carmelita spirituality:

The book records the spiritual struggles of Fr. Tracy as he attempts to respond to pastoral challenges in a post-Vatican II era. While honest in its assessment of successes and failure, the book reveals the prophetic and prayerful heart of a Carmelite. It was *there all along.*

Frank Monahan, retired lobbyist for U.S. Bishops in Washington, DC., for thirty years:

Tracy O'Sullivan, whom I have known since he was a student in the 1950's, writes about his work as a Carmelite priest in the ghettoes of Chicago and Los Angeles. He is not just sharing his quest for social justice but is probing the meaning of his life or in his words: "the search for the face of the living God" in his work. It is an important part of the history of the life of the post Vatican II Church in the U.S.

Leopold Glueckert, O. Carm., Carmelite Historian:

As I read Tracy's *Been There All Along*, I reflected that this is a story as good as a good novel, and better than many. He ruthlessly exposes his own struggles with inner and outer demons. Whether closing down ghetto saloons, or fighting back against his own dance with alcohol, he stays focused on the need to maintain a spiritual and prayerful dimension. He effectively shows how to ignore the wind, fire, and earthquake in favor of listening to the gentle, whispering sound which forms part of the Carmelite's most important journey.

Kevin Burke, CEO, Trinity Capital

Father Tracy O'Sullivan is a throwback to the Middle Ages when the local Catholic priest was the only thing standing between the gentry gobbling up all the property in a village and the poor parishioners who made everything work. A tireless advocate of his parishioners and anyone else in the community, he is both a confessor and a protector as well as a staunch believer that there is no evangelization without social action -which is exactly what the Holy Father, Pope Francis is saying now! The book is a fantastic read

Been There All Along

Tracy O'Sullivan, O. Carm.

Carmelite Media

Layout and Cover Design by William J. Harry, O. Carm.

Carmelite Media
8501 Bailey Road
Darien, Illinois 60561

Phone: 1-630-971-0724
Email: publications@carmelitemedia.org
Website: carmelites.info/publications

ISBN: 978-1-936742-08-0

TABLE OF CONTENTS

I would like to thank Fr. David Blanchard, O. Carm., and Dr. Philip Kenny, Ph.D., for their significant editorial help.

x -

INTRODUCTION

This is my story. I want to tell of my journey to walk with Jesus in the particular role as priest and Carmelite in the post Vatican II era. My purpose is to recount events from the late twentieth century history of the Carmelite Province of the Most Pure Heart of Mary; events that I played a part in defining. My reason for writing is that through participation in these events and reflecting on them, I came to understand my Carmelite and priestly vocation in ways that eluded me in my more structured formation. Although a biography, this essay is also styled to be a theological reflection on fifty years of ministry.

In *Biography as Theology* James McClendon writes, "there is no foundational truth available apart from actual life, no set of timeless premises acceptable to believers and non- believers alike, upon which Christian theology can once and for all found its doctrines."[1] I agree with McClendon and would argue that all of theology must be read and considered within its larger historical framework, including biography. History and biography are necessary for the performance of any theology that confesses that Jesus Christ is the only Son of the Living God and that He lived, breathed, walked, and loved in a particular time.

Biography and autobiography assume the structure of narrative. This narrative of my life as a Carmelite and a priest draws together episodes that might appear otherwise disparate. I chose the episodes that form this narrative as a way to unite other contingencies, including episodes from the life our province, the Church, and events involving other persons. Taken alone every element of narrative is of interest only if it is surprising. But when woven into a life, a drama, and a plot these surprises appear necessary. They reveal the mystery of God working in our lives.

Narratives are made up of actions and events but also of characters and personalities. Plots relate the mutual development of a story and a character or set of characters. Every character in a story of any complexity both acts and is acted upon. Finally, a narrative's characters only rise to the status of persons — fictional or real — who can initiate action when one evaluates their doings and sufferings and imputes them to the actors and victims as praiseworthy or otherwise. One evaluates how the person responds when confronted by another living being who is in some need that the person can address.

In sum, a narrative about human persons tells of both the connections that unify multiple actions over a span of time performed, in most cases, by a multiplicity of persons and the connections that link multiple viewpoints and assessments of those actions. I have experienced this in my life and my intention is to share that autobiographical narrative with others who are on the same road to self discovery as a follower of Christ in the post Vatican II world. My discovery of myself as priest and more so as a Carmelite ultimately find meaning in the question of Jesus, "Who do you say I am?"

I had quite a run as a young, activist priest in the Woodlawn area on the South Side of Chicago. Six years (1964-70) of seeking change and progress were both fruitful, and frustrating. Reality was a lot denser than all of my good will and enthusiastic energy. One step forward and two backward was more the pattern than my youthful dreams of changing the world for good.

One day in 1970 I stopped my frenetic activity long enough to realize I had become confused and bewildered. This realization was a new experience for me. I did not understand at the time, but it was the end of the sixties for me. It had been a glorious ride where we were always just one more press conference away from the coming of the Kingdom.

The sixties left me with a lot more questions than answers. As I entered the 1970s these problems began to penetrate the depths of my soul. I was one confused crusader. My fondest hopes for change in society and the Church were crumbling. More deeply, I felt empty. I wanted to give up the struggle but I just could not.

My world was collapsing on all sides. Most of my friends from the seminary were leaving the priesthood. The Cardinal of Chicago had me on his short list of priests he would like to see leave his archdiocese. The cry from some of the most vocal in the Black community was, "Whitey go home!" Besides that, I was alienated from most of my white friends and on thin ice with my family.

I had stopped praying and started drinking which is a bad combination. Energy for new crusades was riding on an empty tank. There was, however, one small light in my valley of darkness. I had the beautiful experience of walking with many Black individuals and families locked into the ghetto who stayed faithful to the consuming struggle for their dignity and, most of all, a better life for their children.

One morning, I began the passage out of that particular darkness. There were many more to come. I determined that I was going to plunge into life as I encountered it. The decision did not eliminate my confusion. It was a bit terrifying but it set me on the road to be free of the dark hopelessness that was killing me.

Many years later, I read a passage from one of my Carmelite brothers, Jack Welch, which came close to describing my crisis.

"The core value at all times in Carmelite history has been that mysterious Presence met deep within searching lives. Carmelites have left a trail of structures and literature born out of engagement with that Presence. The ways of organizing Carmel's life have been multiple...

The external structures are meant to assist an internal journey which Carmel's literature has imaged in various ways: among them, a journey through a castle, traveling a "little way," passage through a dark night, a search for the beloved in mountain pastures. The last image recalls where it all began."[2]

That commitment to seek life was related to the Presence that has been part of our Carmelite journey. It would take most of the rest of my life to discover that I was on the right path. Being a Carmelite was nowhere in my consciousness at that time. However, I would learn that it was going to crescendo to be the dominating reality of my life. That moment was one of many times I was searching for God only to learn, ever so slowly, God has "been there all along!"

This is the story of that journey to discover my Carmelite calling. In more than a few ways, it is the story of many in my generation who struggled to understand the prophetic voice of Vatican II on the run rather than in a more organized way. In my early years, my calling as a Carmelite religious was vague, if not superficial. Over time, I would learn that the Carmelite calling, to search for the face of the living God, was at the center of my being.

I would like to go to the middle to start this story of my journey to be a Carmelite, a searcher for God. I had just finished twenty-five intense, challenging, and very fulfilling years on the South Side of Chicago. I was beginning a five year assignment as head of the seminary for the Carmelites in Washington, DC. I had returned to Chicago to receive an award from the Chicago Call to Action, a strong voice for progressive change in the Church. Msgr. Jack Egan, a legendary urban minister and the most visible pioneer of the Chicago Church's effort to serve the poor, presented the award that Friday night, November 24, 1989.

"Tracy, you are not an ordinary guy, not an ordinary Carmelite priest.

I can say the usual things about you as we present this award to you....I have found you a faithful, loyal priest who set your eyes to the task and never looked back, but looked ahead to the next hill to be climbed.

Everybody here knows that you served in Woodlawn and called the shots as you saw them. When you encountered a bunch of bastards ripping off the people, you got angry and they tasted the white hot anger of your soul.

You saw the Lord in the people of the area where you lived and worked. We know that the housing of homeless mothers and unwed mothers was of special concern to you and so you gave every encouragement to the women –religious and lay – who gave their best in time, talent, and substance to care for them, and you gave your unqualified support to the work.

Is there a person here who does not remember your fight with the gangs, with the pimps, the drug-pushers, with Jackson Park Hospital, with the Archdiocese, with City Hall, with the now disappointing TWO?

We here assembled also know that you reached out to all of Chicago and said, "Come and see. Come and join hands with us…come and sing with us and worship the God who made us all sisters and brothers. One of the other…your flesh and blood is here in Woodlawn, suffering and dying…. come and join us in bringing solace and a piece of yourself, and you will not go away without your soul and your mind being better for the experience.

We know, Tracy, that where there was a human problem, you brought a wealth of wisdom, courage, experience, and toughness to bear to help work with all others – always with them – to solve and ameliorate the situation.

What we did not know as you moved through the years and spent yourself working and consulting and laughing and listening – that all the while you possessed a heart of gold and a spirit of one reaching for the stars… one who saw a vision of what each human being could be if only they were loved and believed in a little bit… it was your heart of gold and your love of God that captivated us, dear friend, and for that reason the wisdom of the Board of the Call to Action is happy to grant you this well-deserved award – the highest tribute they can give for it contains all the love of everybody here and far beyond."

Jack Egan's generous hyperbole captivated me. Still I knew a different story about myself that was a much more real expression of my flawed humanity. The weeds and the wheat were always in full battle readiness in my passage. During the latter part of my engagement in the urban struggle, I was in an escalating personal battle with alcohol.

When I was named pastor of St. Clara-St. Cyril in June 1984, I knew I was a disaster waiting to happen. I tried to stop drinking and I did. It only took me about 200 times to eventually close the deal.

In this struggle, I chose to seek a deeper commitment to the Carmelite life rather than the Alcoholics Anonymous (AA) program. In the end, of course, they are not that much different from one another. Both are an opening to God's grace. A few years later I was moved to see the entire experience in light of Exodus 19:4 "Tell the Israelites: you have seen for yourselves how

1

From "Going My Way" to "On the Waterfront" [3]

Between 1890 and 1920 Chicago had the fastest urban growth in human history. This was exceeded by several cities only at the end of the Second World War. The Windy City went from one million to three million in these thirty years. In 1910 nine of ten residents were either an immigrant or the child of an immigrant. The majority of these newcomers were Catholic.

For the next half century the ethnic diversity of these newcomers was a dominant factor in the social reality of the Windy City. At the beginning, Negroes were a small part of the complex population.

The Catholic Church's pastoral plan was to respect the ethnicity and culture of the many groups, while preparing the children for full participation in the larger society through the Catholic schools. The Church had great success in this plan.

By the 1940s the Negro population in Chicago had grown. It was about to experience an even more explosive expansion over the next few decades. At this time two seminarians approached Cardinal Stritch to seek permission to leave the Archdiocese and to join the Josephites, a group of Catholic priests who were dedicated exclusively to ministry to the Negro community.

Cardinal Stritch was a Southerner from Memphis with sensitivity to the Negro not common in the history of Chicago hierarchy. He had a clear perception that a big demographic transformation was on the horizon. He shared his concern with the young men and promised them full support in working in the Negro community. Fr. Joe Richards and Fr. Martin "Doc" Farrell became legendary leaders in the Archdiocese's ministry to Negroes. They developed a plan, eventually called *The Chicago Plan*, which influenced ministry to Negroes across the urban north in the 1950s and early 1960s.

The plan was simple. Catholics had something Negroes wanted and Negroes offered an opportunity to fill empty schools and parishes for Catholics. The major negotiable was quality education in Catholic schools. In exchange for the cherished opportunity to get quality education for their children, Negro parents had to attend catechism classes in the Catholic faith and attend Mass every Sunday as a family.

The result was many schools and churches were near capacity and great numbers of Negroes joined the Catholic Church. At its zenith in the early sixties, the parishes of Fr. Richards and Fr. Farrell, Holy Angels and Holy Cross, had baptism ceremonies for over a hundred persons several times each year.

The two priests were aggressive in reaching out to any new pastor of a parish that had experienced racial change. There were increasing numbers of these parishes despite the white community's ferocious effort to block the expansion of the ghetto.

I arrived at St. Clara parish in August 1964. I had grown up just a mile away in St. Laurence parish. I was the seventh of eight children of Irish immigrants who came to the south side at the time of the Irish Civil War in 1923. The four boys attended Mt. Carmel and the four girls attended Loretto High just down the street from the Carmelite high school. The once familiar neighborhood was a new reality to me because of its racial change in the previous several years. This area of the city, called Woodlawn, was just south of the University of Chicago. As a young priest, naïve and very enthusiastic, I was excited about the challenge.

Time would reveal that my pastor and I were not only operating in different worlds, but in different galaxies! Fr. Mario Dittami saw his mission very clearly. He was there to pay off a significant debt left by the previous pastor in the chaos of rapid racial change. Fundraising was his specialty and he was up to the task.

He learned that I was not going to be a pliable student for his pastoral vision. He literally told me to spend my time with the school kids on the playground. It was sort of like "Going My Way" in living color. My heart was much more inclined to be the priest in "On the Waterfront".

I enjoyed being with the children. I remember a particular event that exposed the volatile combination of my naiveté and enthusiasm. There was a long tradition in Chicago to dismiss the Catholic school students early on Wednesday afternoon and have the Catholic public school students come to the nuns for an hour of catechetical instruction.

I took on the task of bringing the public school kids over to our parish school. After a few weeks, I had developed quite a following. On the fourth week I thought I had a real coup. I brought over 500 students. It was fulltime bedlam. On another occasion I had a more focused expression of my enthusiasm. I wanted to go to Selma for the historic march. Fr. Mario thought that it was not only expensive but a crazy idea. I used my weekly religion class in fourth grade that day to have a march in the classroom. Thirty-five years later, one of the students told me he remembers that day and still cherishes the experience.

Over the years, I would grow out of the naiveté of how the school operated but maintain the enthusiasm and creativity. For the next few years, my involvement in the daily school operation and administration would be minimal. It would take many years before I truly grasped the power and beauty of inner city Catholic education.

After my arrival at St. Clara's, Fr. Richards invited me out to lunch. Following his advice, I soon was on my way to work out the *Chicago Plan* as much as I could under Fr. Mario's constraints

One area where I did have freedom to operate was the adult catechism classes. To recruit for this program and for the school, I began to go door to door every evening or Saturday that I was free. This proved to be the beginning of my journey into the Black experience. As I listened to the stories, the pain and the injustice of the overcrowding and segregation slowly penetrated my consciousness. I was learning something that would be at the heart of my pastoral work: go to where the pain is.

Going out at night in Woodlawn was not dangerous. There were three reasons. First, the Catholic priest was deeply respected and recognized in the Negro community. Second, the drug problem was minimal and hidden away off the streets. Third, there were few guns, even among the gangs. All that would change in the next few years. The depth and intensity of the social upheaval led me to observe, "You cannot understand the sixties unless you realize that each year was like a decade in terms of social change."

Another change was taking place that would undercut one of the strong foundations of the *Chicago Plan*. In the 1950s and early 1960s Negroes saw Chicago as a Catholic city. Being Catholic helped one advance in the system with upward mobility. While everyone could celebrate the Civil Rights movement in the South, it was a different reality as it reached the North amidst deep unrest, riots, and a growing cry for Black Power. Suddenly, being Black was a lot more urgent than being Catholic.

This was one of many "wind at your back" incidents I experienced over the next several decades. Whether because of demographics, the social atmosphere, or the political situation, there are certain times when a particular program seems to be going well. Then it loses the "wind at its back" character and there is need for adjustment. This was the case with the adult catechism classes.

Not only were fewer people attending, but I felt a great disconnect between the basic Baltimore Catechism approach and my awareness of the harsh injustice of the segregated and overcrowded social conditions of the Woodlawn community. Also, these were the final years of the Vatican Council. While I was a long way from grasping the radical depths we were being called to, I sensed a deep dissatisfaction with my theological vision and tools.

This disconnect led to a conflict. It was between my youthful enthusiasm and the real confusion and unrest in my teaching and preaching. I was a long way from coming close to proclaiming the Gospel. I began to feel like I was only passing on "South Side Irish Tribal Customs." It was going to take me a long time to truly understand what was happening to me.

At the early stages of this journey of understanding, I grasped that what I was teaching and preaching was a white version of the Christian message with a great overlay of South Side Irish culture and worldview that did not speak to my parish community. In my confusion I had moved away from the core message of the Gospel, toward a more socially oriented message, to address the reality of the people's lives but without the core of the Gospel message to focus the goal of the struggle.

I had no idea how important this distortion was at the time. It would play itself out over the next few decades. The issue was enculturation. It required the development of a truly Black and Catholic experience in worship and liturgy, Black leadership and, most importantly, the urgent need for Black priests and bishops. Time would prove that this was to be a painful and not always successful journey. A lot of ego had to die on the way from Irish tribal customs to Gospel music.

This movement toward addressing the harsh reality of Woodlawn just escalated the conflict with my pastor. However, I was not the only one he was having trouble with. The idea of English in the liturgy was an easy target for his almost total rejection of Vatican II's evolving vision.

Then there were the "good Sisters." In 1965 on the feast day of St. Francis, their patron, he gave the nuns a nice statue of St. Francis. He also gave each nun an electric blanket. He told them he was really tight on money, so he would not be able to give them as much heat during the winter.

Six weeks later, the Sisters boldly asked him for a station wagon. They had no car. In the rapidly changing times, this was a growing burden. Fr. Mario was just not able to grasp the true difficulty of the nuns' situation. I helped the nuns to insist on the urgency of their case. This led to a real breakthrough and Fr. Mario did buy the nuns a new station wagon.

In my growing involvement in the community, I began to encounter young kids in the gangs. This was followed by my first of many funerals of youngsters killed in the escalating gang violence. In my first year and a half in the parish, the gangs grew rapidly as result of the overcrowding and few resources for youth. However, there were few guns and the fights were escalating to bats and chains and knives. Drugs were a non-issue on the streets. That all changed rapidly from early 1966 onward.

Another example of social change was the freedom shirt. This was the clerical shirt first worn by those in the Civil Rights struggle in the South. I began wearing one in the summer of 1965. For me this meant a move away from the religious habit and the formal black suit and collar as typical clerical garb.

One day I went over to nearby Mt. Carmel High School in my freedom shirt. I was mocked by several of my Carmelite brothers. By springtime, half of the clerical faculty was wearing freedom shirts. The winds of change were blowing.

The switch to the freedom shirt was rooted in a total complex of changes that were permeating my life. For me, and for my generation, especially women religious, the habit was a symbol of the many expressions of meaningless and sometime destructive practices in religious life that had been passed on without reflection for centuries. Whatever the renewal of religious life would bring in the immediate future, many of us felt that the religious habit was a symbol of the past.

Another change that burst onto the scene was the theme of the Servant Church. It put the emphasis on service that responded to the urgent needs of the people. It stressed the Christian witness of love and service in the midst of the social turmoil of the ghetto. It proclaimed a message of hope in the Risen Christ. Its emphasis was more on Christian life than maintenance of the Catholic institutions that was central to the *Chicago Plan*. This Servant model clashed with the *Chicago Plan*. The conflict generated a liberal versus conservative or young versus old paradigm. In fact, both approaches had much to offer, but, in the heat of rapid change and with a lack of leadership, the pastoral approach in the increasing number of racially changing parishes became unclear. Only the strong voice of Black leadership a few years later would bring some clarity and direction to the basic vision for the new reality of the Black Catholic parish and school. A great opportunity was severely diminished in the process.

In July 1966, both Fr. Mario and I left St. Clara. He went on to be the director of our foreign mission program where he did a great job for a long time. I was transferred to St. Cyril, a parish just a few blocks to the east right next to Mt. Carmel High School. Fr Bellarmine Wilson was newly named pastor after four years as associate pastor. He was a determined and enthusiastic young man. He was glad to have me and assigned me to work in community activities as my main ministry.

Just when I was beginning at St. Cyril, a new archbishop arrived in Chicago. The soon to be cardinal, John Cody, started a seventeen year term of continual controversy. One of his first moves was to remove Msgr. Jack Egan as head of the Office of Urban Affairs. At this time the work of Msgr. Egan supplied both great influence and vision for multiple projects for the betterment of the poor. Housing in poor communities was a particular thrust of his efforts.

One of these projects was meant to take place at St. Cyril. Fr. Bellarmine had been working on it for a few years and was ready to sign a contract that would allow him to put a shovel in the ground. This would develop three square blocks with new and affordable housing.

The new archbishop did not want anything to do with housing. He appointed a recently returned professor of Canon Law in Rome as his Co-Chancellor. Fr. Ed Egan became Cardinal Cody's man for urban affairs and, among other things he closed down almost all of Msgr. Jack Egan's projects including the St Cyril venture.[4] Fr. Bellarmine was crushed after seeing many years of work and dreams snuffed out with no possibility of dialogue. It was over in a phone call.

Meanwhile, I was off and running in other projects in the community. The Woodlawn Pastors' Alliance was deeply concerned about a particularly outrageous situation that was right in the heart of St. Cyril parish. There were thirteen taverns and two liquor stores on the north side of a block and half of 63rd St. It was called Skid Row.

The police response to the on-going problem was what was called an "umbrella car". The police car was there twenty-four hours a day. The crew changed but the car stayed ready for the action. There was plenty of action to attend to.

I took on the project that had frustrated pastors and community members for years. There was a law in Chicago that an individual voting precinct could vote itself dry. I quietly proceeded to get enough signatures to put it on the ballot.

This vote ultimately involved a lot of money. The most powerful columnist in Chicago, Mike Royko, wrote a column to show the figures and to conclude this was a futile effort. His column made the upcoming precinct election a very public issue.

The liquor industry brought out their high powered lawyers to get the issue off the ballot by challenging the signatures. Before I started the work, I had had some high class legal advice of my own on the legal niceties of collecting the signatures. I was very careful to follow their advice. Still, it was not certain we would survive their high-powered challenge.

The Woodlawn Organization (TWO)[5] saw this project as a loser so gave it no support. Now, however, the publicity of Royko's column brought out all the TV stations and other papers. TWO had to buy in. On the Saturday before the court date, TWO organized a huge rally. Thousands of signatures were collected and presented to Mayor Daley.

On the following Monday, we brought three busloads of people to the court hearing. The Clerk of the Court called me out of the crowd to tell me we had won. Mayor Daley had spoken. Often in Chicago legal niceties were determined by a phone call from Mayor Daley to the judge. A month later, we won the election 280-47. Thirteen taverns and two liquor stores disappeared.

Royko wrote another column admitting his shock and I began my fifteen minutes of fame and initiated my "graduate studies" in the politics of Chicago.

Back at the parish, Fr. Bellarmine developed what seemed like a chronic cough. After seeing a doctor, he was diagnosed with pericarditis, an inflammation in the sac around the heart. I was alone in the parish from April to August in 1967.

That summer we faced a very volatile situation in the inner cities of the nation. Many riots eventually erupted.

For the first time federal money was available to address the unemployed youth. I developed a summer program that targeted both the teens and the younger children. Eventually, it had ten adult volunteers, twelve seminarians, one hundred ten teen Neighborhood Youth Workers, local teens who were paid for their services, and about five hundred children. It was a formula for chaos to have such a large program in our small facilities without a well-organized program. Somehow we stumbled along and eventually helped a lot of people. We kept a great number of people busy and some even learned something. We also brought a good deal of income into many desperate families.

However, there was a problem with the leadership of the powerful gang in the neighborhood, the Black P Stone Nation. Most of the workers in our teen program were members of the Conservatives, one of many sub-gangs that had consolidated into the Black P Stone Nation. They were too independent for the leadership. One day I received notice from the gang leaders that our program was closed down until further notice. While closing the program was a total disaster for me, it was the prudent choice, and I did it.

I proceeded to meet with Jeff Fort and Gene Hariston, the leaders of the

Black P Stone Nation, to discuss the situation. They felt the program was chaotic and they had a solution. They wanted one of their top men to come in as director of the teen workers. I needed help in this area and this made sense to me and we moved out of the shut down quickly.

Gene had a memorandum of agreement that said over dramatically and incorrectly, "Tracy has agreed to hand over the St. Cyril program to us." The Gang Intelligence, a unit of the Police Department, confiscated the document and passed it on to Cardinal Cody. The cardinal gave it to Msgr. Cook who was in charge to Catholic Charities, the agency that funneled the federal funds to our program. Cardinal Cody's message was to get rid of that Fr. O'Sullivan.

That was my lucky day.

When the cardinal arrived, he quickly centralized the funds of all the Archdiocesan programs and agencies under his immediate control. Msgr. Cook was a holdout, and was furious with the new archbishop.

He gave me a sympathetic ear and understood that I had not handed over the program but had accepted reasonable help in a difficult situation. So we survived that crisis and, in fact, through the jobs, brought a great deal of money into the community that was in need of all the help it could get.

While I had some grasp of the complexity of the gang situation, events were going to show how few people understood the depth of the violence that was to evolve over the next few years. The leader who came into our program was called "Watusi." His real name was Charles Rose. In the summer of 1968 he would be the key witness in a Senate investigation of the Black P Stone Nation. He was assassinated on Christmas 1968. In September 1968, eight members of the rebellious Conservatives were killed in separate incidents. A few years later, the leadership issue was settled with the assassination of Gene Hariston.

2

Fifteen Minutes of Fame

The success of the Skid Row vote and the ensuing publicity had big consequences in my life. I became a public figure and quickly was engulfed in my "fifteen minutes of fame." I loved it.

I began working with the Civil Rights Committee of The Woodlawn Organization. Soon enough I was the co-chair and creating a very dynamic agenda in health care, police brutality, and the gangs.

My rise was taking place in the midst of some of the most intense political and social change in the years from 1966 to 1971. Vietnam had escalated from a small military intervention to a program whose cost and commitment of over 50,000 American lives that almost tore asunder the fabric unifying our nation. I was very slow to grasp this reality because of the blinding intensity of the reality in Woodlawn. I remember becoming very angry when Dr. King came out against the war in 1967. I considered it a foolish move away from the urgent issue of the Black struggle. Shortly afterward my eyes and my heart opened to his wisdom.

Dr. King moved into Chicago in late 1965. His arrival escalated the racial tension of the city to an all-time high. Dr. King's agenda was integration in housing. Mayor Daley so outmaneuvered him politically that, in the end, the great civil rights leader was looking for any way to leave Chicago that would save face.

Mayor Daley's victory led to the most segregated city in the nation to this day. Riots devastated Detroit and Newark and frightened Chicago in 1967. Dr. King's death in 1968 led to a massive increase in the depth and breadth of the riots. Mayor Daley responded with his notorious "Shoot to kill!" mandate. Five thousand troops bivouacked in our parish in Jackson Park that April of 1968. Finally, Bobby Kennedy's assassination, in June 1968, ended hope of some progressive resolution of the growing chaos.

The August 1968 Democratic Convention, held in Chicago was another shameful event in our country's history. During the Convention Jackson Park hosted 10,000 troops.

In 1968 the number of Catholic seminarians declined by 50 percent. This was mostly due to the closing of almost all high school seminaries but it was a sign of change that continues. The decline of is even more dramatic. Cassius Clay changed his name to Muhammad Ali and became a conscientious objector. He spent a great deal of time in Woodlawn during the five years he was out of the ring.

A good example of the speed and depth of the change in my role in the community was a meeting in Mayor Daley's office. Less than two years after I led an enactment of the Selma march in my fourth grade religion class, I also led a delegation of Woodlawn pastors to negotiate with the mayor about the issuance of liquor licenses in our community.

My role as a leader of TWO's Civil Rights Committee brought me into confrontational situations with the political and legal leaders in Chicago in a span of two and a half years. I led a delegation in three confrontational meetings with the superintendent of police; organized witnesses for two coroner inquest hearings; testified before two grand juries; met with our Congressman, the editorial boards of the local newspapers, and the District Attorney frequently; together with the assistant United States attorney we setup a task force on police brutality.

The first Carmelites were Crusaders over 800 years ago before they retired to become men of prayer on Mt. Carmel. This was my time of Crusades. I want to share some of the powerful and personal moments of these projects.

The First Crusade: The Case of Officer Fine

The Civil Rights Committee had taken on several cases of police brutality including the death of a teenager, Kenneth Alexander, who was shot in the back. This effort was received with warm support in the Black community and great hostility in the white community.

One morning I received an anonymous phone call that described how a Black man, Eldridge Gaston, had been hit over the head while spread-eagled at the side of his car after a traffic violation. I was told he died the next morning at the Cook County Hospital after a short stay at Jackson Park Hospital. The altercation took place in front of Jackson Park Hospital and had been witnessed by several people in a near-by bar who had simply looked out the window to catch the action when they saw the familiar blue lights of the squad car.

I spent several days working as an investigator to put the pieces together. I had a strong case and I knew what to do with it. I had been invited by the US Attorney's Office to bring them any good cases we surfaced on police brutality. They had the power of a recently amended Civil Rights law that covered this area and they wanted to get the message out.

In the investigation leading up to the indictment, it surfaced that the officer, Joseph Fine, had falsified his employment application. He had denied that he had been under psychiatric residential care.

Although several Black witnesses testified that they had seen Officer Fine hit Gaston over the head with a club, the officer denied it and said there was an altercation. His lawyer told the all white jury in a courtroom filled with police personnel that if the police officer was found guilty no police officer in Chicago would be able to do their job. The jury deliberated for forty-five minutes and came to a not guilty verdict.

Immediately after the verdict was announced, Judge Bernard Decker called Fine before him and said the following, "Any police officer who makes an unprovoked attack on a motorist stopped for speeding deserves to be indicted and prosecuted."

"The jury has concluded that the prosecution did not prove your guilt beyond a reasonable doubt."

"You should not, and no policeman should interpret this, as condoning this type of conduct."[6]

This trial had a bad mix of factors for a 1969 Chicago caught in the tightening vice of racial hostility. The officer was white. The victim was black as were all the witnesses.

It was one of the sadder days of many sad days for me during at this time.

The Second Crusade: Jackson Park Hospital

One of the many changes in Woodlawn at the time of the rapid turnover from White to Black was the loss of medical services. The neighborhood's population had more than doubled but the number of doctors went from thirty-six to nine. This drop put incredible pressure on the emergency rooms of the local hospitals. The general pattern of health care for the poor was fragmented, not easily accessible either in time or place, often impersonal and rude, and required proofs of eligibility which were both arbitrary and confusing. The accumulation of these factors added to the growing pressure of life in the ghetto.

The Civil Rights Committee initially began to address this deep and pervasive problem of health care in a dialogue with the local hospitals. One of the hospitals, Jackson Park, was openly hostile to our approach from day one. That hostility allowed us to bring the public spotlight on the problem of health care for the poor. However, as events developed over the next eighteen months, my involvement slowly evolved into a personal obsession. Health care for the poor slowly got transformed, in my mind, to Fr. Tracy the good guy vs. Dr. Morris Friedell, the almost singular financial beneficiary of Jackson Park, as the really bad guy.

After several failed attempts to negotiate, the TWO Civil Rights Committee had two events that brought a great deal of public attention to the issue. In early December 1967, it had a large demonstration of more than 200 people in front of the hospital. Two weeks later, the group took over the stage of a downtown hotel at a national meeting of the American Medical Association (AMA) on care for the poor. We made the case against Jackson Park. In the spirit of revolt at the time, the AMA let us get away with the gross violation of their hospitality. We got great coverage including national TV.

These public actions led to one of the acquaintances of Dr. Friedell, who was the owner and director of Jackson Park, to anticipate the pattern of "Deep Throat" of Watergate fame, in a clandestine meeting one evening. At 10:30 one night, I was called and asked if I wanted to know the real story about Dr. Friedell. I left my house and headed out to a northern suburb to get the story.

The meeting produced an entirely new and explosive message about the doctor's control of all the sources of revenue and levers of power at the institution for his incredible personal financial benefit. Dr. Friedell purchased the hospital, made it non-profit, and then established a foundation and board that was woven into a single unit driven by nepotism and financial self-interest. One member of the board was Dr. Friedell's father-in-law, Dr. Morris Fishbein, who had been the longtime dominating voice of the American Medical Association. At the time he was a medical expert shilling the minimal health consequences of smoking for the tobacco industry. The financial exploitation of the poor in terms of high prices, selective services, and low wages fed the money machine. Also included in the process was the purchase of property and materials in a way to increase the profit. Even the presence of doctors on the staff worked to enhance Dr. Friedell's control. He manipulated their hidden foibles and addictions to his benefit. For example, he had a doctor beholden to him take the fall, when he, Dr. Friedell, left a surgical sponge inside the body of a patient.

After we digested and organized this "Deep Throat" bonanza of information we began a new wave of publicity against Jackson Park Hospital. We refocused the attack to highlight the exploitation of the poor as the basis of the complaints. One case I remember well. Mrs. Martha Jones brought her elderly husband into the emergency room at Jackson Park. To increase profit the hospital rejected almost all Medicare cases. The couple was shipped in a police paddy wagon to County Hospital about fifteen miles away. No recommendation of medical urgency was given. The husband died in her arms twelve hours later, waiting for service. Mrs. Jones told me, "The hardest part of it all was the trip in the police wagon. They wrapped him in a urine drenched blanket that they would not use on a dog."

Eventually, several city agencies demanded clarification from the hospital. The biggest threat was to its non-profit status. This was investigated by the Attorney General. In the end Dr. Friedell limped across the victory line.

The apparent failure of Crusade II blinded me to a contribution we had made to address the problem of medical care for the poor. We had surfaced the issue in the public's eye with drama and passion. The campaign resulted in the expansion of emergency services in the area hospitals including a new and larger emergency room at Jackson Park. There were also several new health clinics created in our community.

The Third Crusade: The Gangs

Crusade III was with the gangs. My involvement with this explosive issue was more tangential. The main effort was the work of our neighbor, Rev. John Fry of the First Presbyterian Church. He offered a radical approach of almost unquestioning acceptance and support of the leadership of the Black P Stone Nation. He was able to acquire resources to back his vision.

Mayor Daley feared two groups in the Black community: the Black Panthers and the Black P Stone Nation. Both were destroyed by political and police action in the late sixties.

I had a positive experience with the leader of the Black P Stone Nation on the morning of April 5, 1968. I was on my way to talk to the children in our parish school about the death of Dr. King the night before. I met some of our teenage graduates leaving Mt. Carmel High School across the street from our school. They told me that all the Black students walked out when the administration would not have a Mass for Dr. King although the school did in fact have a Mass. Just then, we heard the sound of a mob breaking windows and screaming. At that moment, Jeff Fort arrived in a car saying he might need the basement of our school.

The students from the near-by public high school, Hyde Park, had formed a mob. They were on their way to attack Mt. Carmel. Jeff Fort immediately understood that ultimately such a Black/White confrontation was a losing proposition for the Black community. He proceeded to get the word out that all his gang members were to get out of the rampaging mob and go to a corner lot a block away.

People from the apartments were offering encouragement to the enraged students. When the gang members left, only girls remained in the student faction. They had no plan of attack and remained on the street screaming racial epithets.

The police arrived but in far fewer numbers than the scene warranted because large parts of the city were in a similar simultaneous eruption. The massive upheaval would last for three intense days.

The police misread the intentions of the gang members who gathered on the corner lot. The gang moved, en masse, over 500 at this time, into the recreational center in the basement of our parish school.

Jeff used violence to subdue the raging anger of the group. Eventually two of the revolting gang members had to go to the hospital. Within forty minutes Jeff organized a plan of attack. A strategy and the discipline to make the gang the winners was the result. I helped in negotiations with Mt. Carmel. It ultimately led to some great street theatre which avoided a dimension of racial violence that would have produced a much greater cost of life, and quite likely, deep racial warfare. It is hard to imagine what the deaths of any white students at Mt. Carmel would have meant that early in the equation of a very violent weekend. It had the possibility of contributing to the violence in geometric proportions.

As the drama escalated, Mt. Carmel ordered city buses to vacate the total student body. As the buses departed, the Black P Stone members lined up single file with Jeff Fort sitting on the top of a mail box directing the actions. The gang members gave their Black P Stone Nation salute to each bus. The police stood by relieved, cautious, and disgusted. When all the buses had left, the Black teens snaked danced down the street to their headquarters two blocks away at the First Presbyterian church. This was only one chapter in a book filled with drama and surprises for the Woodlawn community and the Black P Stone Nation that weekend.

For the rest of the weekend, they worked their territory and kept all violence and fires and looting away. This expression of power and control, singular in the Black community that destructive weekend, at first gained wide recognition and praise. The backlash, led by the Gang Intelligence Unit of the Police Department, was fierce and effective. This positive image and potential political power was not acceptable in Mayor Daley's Chicago. Within eighteen months the leaders were in prison and the gang was out of Woodlawn and moving towards an evolution to a much more isolated and sect-like group called the El Rukun.

Two other events capture the sheer craziness of these times.

Good Friday in 1969 was on the first anniversary of Dr. King's death. I returned to the rectory at about 8:30 PM after the liturgy. I received an urgent phone call from a parishioner that her son Roger had been in an accident and wanted to see me as soon as possible. He was in a suburban hospital.

I had to exit the expressway at 95th Street. There was a housing project nearby. I was struck by the absence of cars. Then I learned why. I saw a man with a rifle aiming right at me from the housing project. I stepped on the gas and saved my life. The bullet went through the back side window right behind my head. I went full speed for a mile till I saw a police car parked in front of a fire station. The officer said they were experiencing a good deal of sniper activity and were stretched out so he had to stay to protect the firemen on their runs.

I went five miles more with no problem because it was a white area. But that became my problem as soon as I approached the emergency room. There was a white crowd outside the emergency room. They were both apprehensive and angry. I soon learned why and made sure I left by a different way.

My parishioner really did not have sacramental absolution on his mind. He thought I could save him from being lynched by that crowd. He had grossly overestimated my prowess. That kind of salvation was far above my pay scale.

His story was straightforward and ugly. He had been driving and drinking, which is bad any time, but he upped the ante. He was a young Black man in a white suburb driving under the influence. He lost control of the car and went up on the sidewalk and hit a five-year-old girl who was not expected to live.

The young man's mother was a committed Catholic struggling with the mystery of good and evil in her family. She had two sons who played out the classic story of the good seed and the bad seed. One son, Thomas, was a wonderful young man and eventually had a successful life. Roger spent a lifetime of breaking his mother's heart.

Some years later I saw a small story in the morning *Tribune* about a burglar being shot in a nearby neighborhood. The man was entering a bedroom window only to be greeted by a father with a gun protecting his wife and family. The burglar died on the spot. It was Roger bringing the bad seed to the hands of a merciful God.

I want to share one more public episode that resulted from my Crusades. On St. Patrick's Day, 1971, I was attending Jesse Jackson's Operation Push meeting and rally, a weekly Saturday morning event. Fr. George Clements, a friend and active Black priest in Chicago, asked me to join him for the afternoon. There was going to be a small, symbolic event by the African American Patrolmen's League. They were going to pour black ink into the lagoon in Washington Park which was close to my parish. I told George I was happy to join him.

The event was simple enough. There was a parade of cars driving through the park. At the end, we went to the lagoon and poured black ink into the water. The power of the symbolic action contrasted to the big St. Patrick Day's parade taking place downtown at the same time with the Chicago River dyed green for the event.

The African American Patrolmen's League was looking for recognition which Mayor Daley had denied. He had, in fact, assigned the head of the group to guard the alley behind the main police station on 11th Street so he could not be in any protests during the St. Patrick Parade.

What I did not know beforehand was that Fr. Clements saw me as a further symbol to spice up the protest. I was placed in the lead car, a convertible, alongside the second in command of the Patrolmen's League. Fr. Clements was on the other side. The press also saw the symbolism of a Fr. Tracy O'Sullivan being at the wrong St. Patrick's Day event. I got more coverage than Mayor Daley.

That night it seemed that every drunken Irishman in Chicago called me to share his disgust at my betrayal of my Irish heritage. The calls kept coming for weeks.

3

Leading a Post Vatican II Parish: First Order of Things

In September 1966, the Carmelites had two neighboring parishes in Woodlawn, St. Clara and St. Cyril. They both enjoyed a fairly large participation and the two schools had waiting lists. The Carmelites had staffed both parishes for over sixty years. The School Sisters of St. Francis and the Loretto Sisters served the schools of St. Clara and St Cyril respectively.

In August 1966, a petite, young, first grade nun arrived at St. Cyril School. She was beginning a legendary term of ministry in Woodlawn that continues to today, almost half a century later. Her name is Sister Therese O'Sullivan, IBVM. She transcended both parishes and schools in her ministry. We served together as brother and sister for 22 years.

In September 1966, Fr. Bellarmine Wilson was pastor of St. Cyril. The parish participated in some monumental change in the five years to September 1971, and he was expected to have a key role. In fact he did not function very well.

As I wrote earlier, Bellarmine had received a crushing blow shortly after his pastorate began when he learned that his dream of renovating three square blocks of the parish had been squashed by Cardinal Cody. The disappointment was crushing and he never recovered the fire of his enthusiasm that characterized his four years as associate pastor.

This rejection was quickly followed by a severe illness that necessitated a four month sick leave but which, in fact, was the beginning of his total withdrawal from the parish. This, in turn, led to his third obstacle to stable ministry. He fell in love with the first grade nun at St. Clara.

In March 1968, I returned home one day and Fr. George O'Keefe, one of the five priests we had ministering at both parishes, looked very distressed. He told me that we had to close St. Clara School. Fr. Bellarmine had informed the staff that we had funds for only six more weeks.

At the time, I was completely uninvolved with any parish or school administration but this crisis was the beginning of a journey for me. The God of surprises had a big one in store for me. I was being called off the streets to administer a wild ride, to usher the parishes and schools into a new reality.

In addition to the unprecedented changes in society, the next few years were going to unveil extraordinary fluctuations in the parishes and schools because of the post Vatican II turmoil in the Church and a dramatic population shift in the local community. It was a hectic journey. My initial effort at administration was troublesome. More often than not, I had the subtlety of a blacksmith rather than the gentle touch of the surgeon.

My first task was to undo the blunder of the announcement that St. Clara school was closing. I met with Bellarmine and pointed out that we had a convent fund of $40,000. He said we were not able to use it. I pointed out that we would not need a convent if we did not have a school. This crisis was over for the time!

In January 1968, the priests from St. Cyril moved into the rectory at St. Clara. Fr. Bellarmine was named pastor of both parishes. Fr. Bob Muller and Fr. George O'Keefe were part of the priest team to be joined by Fr. Damon Kelly a few months later. Both parishes maintained their separate identity.

Bi-parish reorganization was a bit chaotic. In March 1968, parish councils were established for both parishes and in September 1969, we established one joint parish council to guide both parishes. Later, in January 1970, we amalgamated the two parishes into one, St. Clara-St. Cyril and in September 1970 we merged both schools into one, St. Cyril. The St. Clara church was used for worship and the St. Cyril School was the location for the merged school.

This tremendous change would have been difficult in the most stable of times and with clear pastoral leadership. We were caught in social and racial turmoil. The changes in the local community were dramatic and correctly described as the biggest turnover in one area of the city since the Chicago Fire. Then there was the turmoil in religious life which deeply affected many individuals on the staff. The School Sisters of St. Francis announced their corporate withdrawal in December 1969, effective June 1970. To add to the chaos, the canonical pastor, Fr. Bellarmine, was practically absent in 1968 and 1969 because of emotional stress.

All of these factors played themselves out slowly at first but then led to rapid and tumultuous changes. Between the two groups of nuns, more than 120 years of service were effectively terminated in one meeting when a Black layman was hired as principal. The new school carried over only four teachers from the twenty that had worked in the two schools. Enrollment slid from 560 to 280 in two years. A proportionate number of parishioners departed for many reasons including the depth and breadth of the changes. No doubt the biggest and most dramatic change was that eighteen of the twenty nuns in the schools left Woodlawn and eleven of these left religious life within a few years. Three of the five priests left the parish and all three left religious life.

It took a Jewish psychologist from New York to help us survive with a modicum of sanity. Dr. Sheldon Schiff came to Woodlawn in 1965. He and his partner, Dr. Smith, began a program of mental health sponsored by the University of Chicago. In the simplest terms, they were trying to create the equivalent of a vaccination shot for mental health for the first grade children. They worked in twelve schools of Woodlawn.

Dr. Schiff became a friend and mentor for me in these difficult years. He had real love for and commitment to our work in the parishes and schools.

Dr. Schiff kept a steady pressure on me to withdraw as a public figure. He said my naiveté was gross. He said no white man should be doing what I was doing in the Civil Rights Committee. As a psychiatrist he knew it would take time for me to grasp that ego-deflating option. At the same time he was tremendously supportive and patient in beckoning me into a healthy reality.

In his interaction with our schools, he became familiar with the disarray of our leadership. Eventually, when it got really bad, he felt free to propose an alternate structure for us. We accepted his idea. It was an Executive Committee, which was given some practical power to act in light of the pastor's withdrawal to nearly total passivity. The Executive Committee would consist of the five priests and the two principals. We were the decision making body. I was the public spokesperson and the *de facto* leader.

The Executive Committee functioned nine months before Bellarmine resigned in June 1969, and left to get married. He remains happily married today.

Fr. George O'Keefe was named pastor. George was a very good friend. George and I worked closely together but George always leaned on me when the pressure came. Working together, we survived the storm and eventually guided the parish and school to a modicum of stability.

In all of this Dr. Schiff was a tremendous source of wisdom and strength until he ran into his own storm that sandbagged his programs in the politics between the University, the TWO, and the larger community.

Black Militant Agenda Arises

Another defining event took place in late January 1969. A group of six Black militants took over a meeting of fifty-two Catholic priests who were working in the Black community. For most of the priests, it was a frightening experience and it led to the departure of many of the priests from service in the Black community over the next several months. The militants' demands were presented as non-negotiable, wrapped in the language of a physical threat. They insisted on a deep commitment to Black control. Likewise, they were adamant in the appointment of Fr. George Clements as pastor of St. Dorothy Parish. The final stipulation was that we have a press conference the next morning to publicly support their agenda.

The *Chicago Plan* was a product of its times. It was wrapped in white paternalism and clericalism. The clear majority of priests that fateful evening were practioners of the *Chicago Plan*. They were confronted with a radial challenge to the validity of their ministry. For some, this involved a major investment of their lives. Their reactions were explosive and divisive: denial, anger, confusion, fear, reluctant acceptance, and, for a few, open support. I had become a true believer in Black Power, and therefore, supportive, yet at the same time, apprehensive.

An older pastor, Fr. John O'Shea, who was very distraught and conflicted about the charges of the militants volunteered to be the spokesman at the press conference. He asked me to stand by to help if necessary.

The next morning we had maximum coverage because the Black militants had leaked a false agenda. The press was expecting us to turn on Cardinal Cody and, even, perhaps, resign from the priesthood.

Fr. John O'Shea lasted about two minutes in front of the cameras. I was on for almost forty-five minutes and held off the headline hunters and kept on message. We supported the development of Black leadership in our parishes and in the Church.

Cardinal Cody totally misunderstood my role in this event and asked for my removal from the archdiocese without a syllable of conversation with me. It was one of five times that my provincial, Fr. Malachy Smith, O. Carm., supported me against the Chicago archbishop who did not want facts to get in the way of his program.

Four months later, a real breakthrough happened. Fr. Clements and three other Black priests were appointed pastors. This assignment of four Black priests as pastors was a historic first in the US Catholic Church.

Meanwhile, back at the parishes in Woodlawn, this challenge of the Black militants and its aftermath had a tremendous impact on our direction. The psychic journey for the priests and nuns seeing ourselves transformed from the saving white angels to the paternalizing white devils was overwhelming, frightening, and uprooting. It proved to be quite a trip that many chose not to take.

At the same time, the leaders in the parish were also in a very different situation. Blacks had seldom been able to have a position of authority. They had practically no experience and minimal training to function as parish council and school board. This added to the heightening tensions between the administration of the parish and school and the lay leaders. We were all floundering. The volatile issue of race made it all the more difficult. On the other hand, most parishioners brought an abundance of good will and openness to the table.

One instance helped me understand our dilemma. I was explaining the urgency of the budget. Decisions have to be related to the resources we have. The issue was crystal clear to me.

However, I could not get the people to stop focusing on a series of concerns and complaints about the school kitchen. We ended up at an impasse that night.

I remember asking one of the sharper women to help me understand. She said it was simple. A $200,000 budget was both foreign and frightening to them. They understood the kitchen. The issues were familiar and manageable in the kitchen.

In spite of all the obstacles, we moved ahead. First, the parish councils absorbed the school boards. Then, after some months, the two parish councils merged. This was a crucial step that paved the way to the merger of the parishes six months later.

The major issue came down to the schools and Black leadership. It was far from a slam dunk. Many of the parents and parishioners did not want a Black principal. Many of the more militant members were adamant that this was the time to have a Black principal in the school. I sided with the latter.

The process of choosing a Black principal ultimately destroyed the structures we had set up. Many people could not handle the depth and intensity of the controversy. The issues became very personal. Finally, there were seven members and two priests left in a meeting that went to 1 AM. We committed to a Black principal. We became the third school in the archdiocese to hire a Black principal.

Looking back, it was the worst decision I supported in my twenty-five years in Woodlawn. While the ideology was pure, the reality proved to be costly in terms of the quality of the school program and it was divisive for the parish.

Here are some of the factors that contributed to my final negative evaluation:

The individual we hired was a hustler in a nice suit. He saw the job as a supplement to his college teaching income. He was gone in five months. The main point here is not that he was a bad choice but that we had little experience in negotiating for a good educator.

His successor was the sixth grade teacher who led the school to the edge of destruction.

The division in the parish and school led to the departure of many good people.

I was thrilled that through a series of maneuvers we were able to obtain programs and rentals that put the new school on a strong economic base for the first time in several years. This meant little when the academic program and the organization of the school fell into complete disorder.

While my sister, Sister Therese and Sister Julie Stapleton stayed, we lost the nuns and their tradition that provided the essential organization of the school and the practice of service. I also want to point out that I was very upset with Fr. Mario and his electric blanket maneuver. It was nothing compared to my blindness in this process with the dismissal of the nuns. The participation and consultation of the nuns was practically non-existent.

All through these years, at the initiation of Dr. Schiff, we were negotiating with some rich benefactors and educators to make our educational program a model of quality education for poor Blacks. It could have meant a reconfiguration of our relationship with the archdiocesan school system. Basically, it could have been a well-funded and well-resourced charter school a couple decades ahead of any of the charter schools of today. It never happened because our internal turmoil consumed us.

Reflection

I had been keeping an incredible pace. It was finally getting to me big time. On March 2, 1971, I wrote the following reflection into my journal:

> I have been very troubled for the last several months and more and more I'm getting a clearer grip on the problem. I'm going to try to put down in words some of the very deep feelings I've been having in the hope that I can clarify the problem.

> First of all, I'll have to admit I'm on the ropes as far as remaining a priest is concerned. This, frankly, is very surprising to me. I never thought I would have doubts about remaining a priest but I must honestly admit I have been seriously considering the option of leaving.

> Secondly, I'm having serious problems with celibacy for the first time. I've always had problems with the obvious attraction of women but I was basically able to handle the scene because I was able to meet needs by work. That is not the case now.

The problem is interwoven in several factors of the change in Woodlawn, the White-Black scene, the theology of the Church, my age at 35, the concept of religious life and the clerical state, and other factors.

It is very sad and disheartening to see Woodlawn washed out and just about any progress we made wiped out. This is a growing factor in my increasing sense of futility.

It also is apparent that we are making progress in the development of Black leadership and this is satisfying. However, I must honestly admit that my personality is not one to stay quiet and in the background. Whether this is something that I can change, it is nevertheless, a factor that *de facto* is frustrating me at this time.

Likewise, I have become increasingly critical of the feasibility of real progress in the institutional Church structure. A heavy price is paid to go along with Cody's game plan. This fits into the overall picture of "Cooling Down of America" led by Nixon. This whole phenomenon, no doubt, is at the base of much of my feeling of frustration and futility.

Another agonizing point is the concept of the clerical state. There are so many points about it that are frustrating to me that it is hard to be conscious of them all. One point is I don't like to be called "Father."

Another area of frustration is the burden of administration that has fallen on my shoulders. This is definitely not my bag. No doubt, if Freeman (the new principal) had panned out, much of this would be off me. I need more freedom to operate and be more myself. This really does not seem possible at the present time.

I am trying to think out the problem…"

Welcome to the Mid-Life Crisis!

"I am trying to think out the problem." I was not into praying with any regularity. That did not stop God. I would soon learn again God had *"been there all along."*

The fiasco of hiring the Black principal led to a change in my fundamental approach. One of the great things about my work as a community organizer was that I had clarity. This gave me power. Confusion or even minimal doubt was not part of my arsenal. It was simple and clear: the historical patterns of prejudice and deprivation made the Black cause good. White was bad. Now, complexity began to creep into my consciousness. It was throwing me off balance.

I did not realize it at the time but I was making the first step to embracing the parable of the weeds and the wheat. This eventually would become a central and dominating image of how I would encounter reality. Here it was starting out as a mustard seed!

A second thought came into the reflections from the pain of my setbacks and frustrations. I was searching for the silver bullet. I wanted a clear, absolute solution. The conquest of Dr. Friedell was not going to be just a victory. It was going to be the solution to the problem of healthcare for the poor. Likewise, the conviction of Officer Fine was not just going to be justice for Eldridge Gaston, the victim, but the beginning of the end of police brutality.

Once you get blinded by your messianic urges, there is no limit to the silver bullets that will end the problem of evil. Of course, our new charter school was going to be the solution to inner city education. My exaggerated grandiosity allowed me the space for some very big dreams.

In the weeds there is always the wheat. The beauty of the situation was that God gave me the grace to dream dreams of a new and richer reality. These dreams, however, had to pass through my exalted ego. God was working to prune down that ego so the dreams could be a little more in tune with God's plans. What I experienced as frustration and loss was just the beginning of God working within me to direct me to a different journey.

I have another phrase that I use often. I say the grace is in the struggle not in the accomplishment. God was sowing the seeds of that in the troubled soil of my heart. It takes us a long time to get on God's agenda even though we always do everything in the name of Jesus! However, most times, we pick our own Jesus, scaled down to our convenience and control, not the Jesus of the Scriptures.

Finally, I would like to tell about three funerals from this time in my life. I was not conscious of it at the time, but the center piece of the midlife crisis is coming to an awareness of our mortality. That awareness was percolating big time underneath the surface in my life.

I was reflecting in my journal about my withdrawal from and growing hostility with the white community. I wrote, "I had to go on a sick call to an old white lady in South Shore. Afterwards, I had to listen to the old white folks complaining about the Negroes. I felt a growing chasm between myself and the white community. The next day I had a funeral of another old white lady that I did not know. I felt it was very functionary. I did not preach because of my inner turmoil on the race issue."

It was more than the race issue. It was my fear of death that was seeping into my consciousness and adding to my turmoil. Now I can see that something deeper was going on here. I did whatever possible to avoid funerals. I hated them. I had a powerful fear of death which was incompatible with my glorious self-image as the crusader so I kept it hidden from myself.

A second funeral was that of my brother-in-law, Jim Heenan. He and my sister Mary had six children. The last was just a few years old when Jim got sick and missed work for the first time ever. Several weeks later the cancer won out and we had his funeral.

This past Christmas, I visited with my oldest sister, Ellen. She shared her memories about the days after Jim's funeral. She went over to Mary's home by bus after she got her seven kids off to school. She tried to get Mary out of bed because the death left her completely overwhelmed and helpless. Mary was facing the responsibility of raising six young kids that included two sets of Irish twins (both born in the same twelve month span) and that would eventually see her with six teenagers at the same time. After seven weeks or so, Mary got out of her bed and became the mother of a fabulous family.

What struck me about Ellen's story was my new awareness that I was oblivious to Mary's crisis. My fear of death prevented me from noticing Mary's suffering.

My father died on May 15, 1971. I celebrated the Mass and preached the homily but did not face the reality of his death. A few years later on a bright fall afternoon I was walking along the lake in Jackson Park. I became agitated about something and suddenly I blurted out, *"Will you get off my back!"* When I finally recognized what I was feeling, I was able to bury my father. I began the process to truly realize that I was going to die. It was the beginning of some true freedom.

One More Crusade

Another event in this period of my life was a conflict with my Carmelite brothers over their neglect of some apartment buildings next to Mt. Carmel High School. The conflict came when several other powerful changes were taking place in the Woodlawn community: a historical population exodus, an unprecedented number of fires, the demise of the Black P Stone Nation, and a growing awareness of the dominance of the University of Chicago in the evolving New Woodlawn.

On October 12, 1971, the headline of the late morning edition of the *Chicago Daily News* read: *Priest Rips Order's Plan for Woodlawn!* The first few paragraphs were even more provocative.

"A Roman Catholic priest in Woodlawn has accused his religious order of forcing Blacks from the community to 'profiteer' in a highly volatile south side neighborhood."

"The priest contends his Order has placed 'property values' above 'human values' by demolishing apartments to make way for the expansion of Mt. Carmel High School.

"He said by doing so the Carmelite Order is playing into the hands of 'racist real estate interests' who want to push the poor from Woodlawn and develop the area for high and middle income families.

"Fr. Tracy O'Sullivan said that instead of demolishing apartment buildings, the Carmelite Order should be building them.

"Fr. O'Sullivan sent a letter out over the weekend to his superiors and all the houses of his province pleading for constructive action in an unstable situation. In the letter, he gave a detailed analysis of the great potential for good or evil in the present circumstances."[7]

That evening, I was called to a meeting with my provincial and his advisory council. After a good discussion the issue was resolved easily. Three things led to what I considered a positive decision. First, I explained that I went public in the *Daily News* to avoid a public demonstration by some community folks in front of Mt. Carmel High. The community activists supported the article and planned to follow up on it if there was not a positive response. Secondly, the council learned for the first time, that the treasurer, one of their own members, had quietly been buying real estate near the school in areas that were easily labeled for speculation. Finally, I had covered my bases in the letter by showing that this action was the logical conclusion of requests and warnings about the volatile situation of the apartment buildings, warnings that had been denied over a period of two years.

We formulated the following press release:

"As a result of charges of Carmelite indifference to housing problems in Woodlawn, a meeting of Carmelite superiors was held Monday evening with Fr. Tracy O'Sullivan, associate pastor of St. Clara parish.

"Fr. Malachy Smith, provincial of the Chicago Carmelites re-affirmed his Order's decision to sponsor low and moderate income housing in the East Woodlawn area earlier this summer. Fr. Smith said, 'Overtures were made to join the Carmelites in co-sponsoring such housing. We re-affirm our pledge and our dedication to the people of Woodlawn. We intend to implement the program with all due speed. As far as Mt. Carmel High School is concerned, we pledge that whatever expansion will be to the mutual advantage of the school and the East Woodlawn area.'"

We developed a plan with local residents and the Carmelites that would include a significant educational component for residents along with affordable housing. We incorporated as a legal entity. We applied for federal funds. After several months, we were rejected by the federal housing agency because such low and moderate income housing did not fit the future plans for such prime real estate.[8]

I want to give a thumbnail sketch of the incredible impact of race on Chicago's housing pattern. This will lead to a much deeper and clearer understanding of what was going on with the Mt. Carmel apartments.

As a child growing up on the South Side of Chicago, I inherited a clearly defined worldview. Race was a strong element of it. I like to describe it this way: *God is good. The sun comes up over the lake. The colored people will never move south of 47th Street. All three premises have equal value! All three came from God!*

The foundational event that produced such a clearly defined view on race was the race riot in 1919. In this riot, Whites killed Negroes and Negroes killed Whites. The death toll was more than thirty. The magnitude of the riot's social and economic impact is hard to comprehend.

After the riot Negroes were given a specific geographical area in which to live. Realtors endorsed a code of ethics not to sell to Negroes in a White area. White homeowners signed a covenant agreement not to sell to Negroes. When these maneuvers failed, violence followed. Chicago averaged a fire bombing once a month at the home of a Black family moving onto a White block not contiguous to the ghetto. This occurred steadily from 1920 to 1975. Chicago had to work to become the most segregated city in the United States and it succeeded.

The problems of maintaining the boundaries of the ghetto were manifold, but none more difficult than sheer numbers. In 1920, the Negro population was 44,000. In 1960, it escalated to 813,000.

So when the area around Mt. Carmel changed from White to Black in the late 1950s, the city was in the beginning stages of a long racial panic.

The Carmelites responded by proposing to expand their campus three blocks east and to add a junior college to their existing school. Their financial campaign, begun in 1956, ultimately failed because the White alumni felt the school could not survive or would become a Black school. However, the financial campaign brought the Carmelites several apartment buildings in the immediate vicinity of the school. These building became problematic in the next several years.

Because of the great influx of Negroes in the 1940s and the early 1950s, the Chicago rule of "block by block" expansion left the Hyde Park neighborhood and the University of Chicago as a natural target of the irreversible expansion of the ghetto. Hyde Park was immediately north of Woodlawn. The city government, the business community, the University, and the Hyde Park community saw this as a potential disaster. They came up with a plan. It was called urban renewal. It was the beginning of a decades long effort to save the University. Everyone in the power structure of Chicago saw this as absolutely essential for the benefit of the city as a whole. The University was a city treasure that had to be protected.

As result of the urban renewal plan, the natural expansion of the ghetto leapfrogged Hyde Park. The impact on Woodlawn, the neighborhood immediately to the south of Hyde Park, was catastrophic. Close to 30,000 new residents came into an unbelievably overcrowded neighborhood in a very short time.

I arrived in Woodlawn as an enthusiastic young priest in August 1964. In the previous five years the population had doubled, rising to 65,000. The number of children increased sevenfold. The city had to build five new elementary schools to join the three already operating. This growth further diminished the strained housing stock. There was great pressure to keep the population contained in the Woodlawn area to protect the adjacent White communities south and west from any further change. As a result, Woodlawn was paying a dear price for the prosperity of Hyde Park.

In this context and with the failure of its plan to expand, Mt. Carmel High School established a policy to maintain the majority White student body while adding a number of Black students. This made Mt. Carmel a rare institution in Chicago at the time, an integrated institution. History has shown this controversial decision was a wise choice.

In the next 25 years, all the girls Catholic high schools on the South Side closed. Two other Catholic boys' high schools, Leo and Hales, survived as Black Catholic high schools but with great difficulty. However, in my last year as pastor, 1989, Mt. Carmel graduated more African American students than either Hales or Leo.

In this overcrowded neighborhood, something deeply frightening was happening. There were an unprecedented number of fires. The fires contributed to a paranoia that fed the community's perception that Mt. Carmel apartments were part of an overall conspiracy to drive them out of Woodlawn.

I tried to get the Woodlawn Organization to publicize the fires but, to my surprise and dismay, they did not want to address the issue. I then moved on my own. I contacted a journalist friend from the *Chicago Daily News*.

His investigation led to a five part, front page series in June 1971, called *The Blitz of Woodlawn*. It documented the series of fires in the Woodlawn area between 1967 and 1971 that had led to the greatest exodus of people from a city community since the Chicago Fire. In 1970 there were 1,600 fires in one square mile of the Woodlawn community. In the short period of four years, 30,000 people had left the community. Those who stayed felt that some powerful conspiracy was in play. They lived in terror of the nightly fires.

The fire department determined that almost all the fires were the result of arson. Amazingly, in the years of the fires only six persons died including one firefighter. East Woodlawn, near Mt. Carmel, was most affected.

4

From the Streets to the Classroom

In late November 1971, Dr. Schiff invited me to lunch. Following our conversation I walked out of the restaurant with a whole new direction in my life. He told me a fight was coming between political forces in the community and The Woodlawn Organization. Basically, TWO had joined forces with the University. Dr. Schiff believed if I stood up publicly in opposition, I would be crushed for something that I simply was not in a position to change. He encouraged a strategic withdrawal.

Dr. Schiff said he personally was caught in the inner workings of the University and that his opposition to the new arrangement made him vulnerable to the loss of his coveted tenure.

Earlier that week, three wonderful and wise mothers, Jesse Nealy, Doris Braggs, and Oresa Gardner had gently but firmly confronted me in a very serious "Come to Jesus" session.

I had been feeling really down, and again was talking about leaving. I was in the midst of a real pity party for Fr. Tracy. They told me that I was a good man and that I could make a meaningful contribution to the effort of the parish and school. They said I first needed to wake up and get real. As Black mothers they were part of the struggle that has been going on for almost four hundred years. They lived daily with the losses, the destruction, the fear, and most of all concern for their children. They had no time for self-pity. So if I wanted to help this is what I could do: become the principal of the parish school and restore it to the quality program that it had been just a few years before. I could then help save their kids and many others.

This was a real blow to my ego at first. Then, I slowly opened up to the possibility. Dr. Schiff helped me seal the deal. He had heard a report of the request earlier in the week from three mothers in the parish that I become principal. He felt it was a very meaningful option for me. He encouraged me to accept this suggestion. When I put my napkin on the table at the end of the meal my "Fifteen Minutes of Fame" were over.

The streets gave way to the classroom.

The Little Red School House

After Christmas 1971, I began a marvelous and joyful part of my life as upper grades language arts teacher and principal of St. Cyril School. I learned that I was a gifted teacher and a fairly decent principal.

By teaching in the morning, I was able to set a very high standard and tone for the entire school. I made it a serious and exciting venture of growth and learning. In a few years, I had the test scores near the national norms. I was able to use contacts throughout the archdiocese to acquire resources that were desperately needed. Second hand books and desks for were as good as new for us.

In the end, most of the kids were on their way to a better life. I learned that Catholic education is an advantage for life.

One day several years later I got a phone call that sort of crystallized my whole venture at St. Cyril School. Pam Nixon, the daughter of our maintenance man, told me she was beginning her internship as a physician at the Cook County Hospital. She called to tell me that another St. Cyril grad, Elton Tyler, the son of our school secretary, was her director in the intern program.

At this time most of my energy was consumed by the school. However, one community project dovetailed with the educational effort.

In April 1974, Cardinal Cody closed four inner city Catholic schools in the neighboring Englewood community. It happened in a shocking way. One afternoon TV news trucks showed up at the schools. For the first time the children, faculty, parents, and, in some cases pastors learned that the schools were in their final month. It was a brutal scene.

We had an emergency meeting of all the inner city priests and principals and many parents. We selected a steering committee to address the crisis. I was selected as co-chairman of the group that included four priests, two principals, and two parents.

We met almost every Saturday morning for eight months. Cardinal Cody resisted any effort we proposed, even the simple process of dialogue. Only with the threat of a public demonstration did he agree to meet us. On the day of the scheduled meeting, we received phone calls directing us to a new and secret site to avoid any press.

At the session the cardinal harangued us for nearly an hour about how complex and difficult it was to maintain all the inner city schools. He then went around the table and challenged each of us personally to come up with a solution for this vexing problem. Each of our members passed until it came to me, the last one on the hot seat. I reported that I had at least part of the solution.

I said that the cardinal should invite all suburban parishes to develop a partnership with the struggling inner city parishes. He blew it off saying that white suburbanites would not help the Black parishes.

I responded that our parish had a very positive sharing program with a suburban parish. It had been operative for several years. I laid out the program with a long list of specifics. He said he would look into it.

A month later the cardinal sent each of the priests at the meeting a personal invitation via registered mail, to attend the Holy Thursday Chrism Mass, the Mass of Unity for priests. I did not attend. It was an ignorant and stubborn and shallow decision on my part.

At the Mass Cardinal Cody announced a fairly significant program for the inner city schools. He promised there would be far ranging consultation and a realistic schedule for the closing of any schools in the future. Then, he surprised everyone by initiating an archdiocesan sharing program which mandated that every parish have at least one sister parish with the goal of meaningful sharing of resources. Even the poorest parishes were asked to make some effort to share with another parish.

This program proved to be a real boon for the Catholic inner city schools over the next fifteen years. It was a meaningful breakthrough on many levels.

The Model

Our parish, St. Clara-St. Cyril, had begun a sharing program with St. Anne in Barrington, 65 miles away. Parishioners on both sides were quite apprehensive at the beginning in 1970 when racial tensions were very strong. We finally agreed to a joint meeting at a neutral site about half way between the two parishes. The slow start gradually picked up steam, in spite of some missteps and misjudgments of what was realistic in our circumstances.

Two leaders eventually arose. Jessie Nealy and Bea Duffy cut through the ice and warmed up the atmosphere to begin a fantastic journey. They set the tone and forged a deep personal friendship. Many other personal relations followed. Over the next 30 years the sharing program produced countless benefits for both parishes.

The key was the leadership that emphasized the people dimension. The financial assistance, which was substantial and helpful, took care of itself.

In the time of its full development there were over twenty people interchanges during the year. These included a regular participation in each other's Sunday liturgies which often saw a great Gospel choir rock the house at St. Anne's. There were joint service projects for the Confirmation classes, exchanges of grade visits in the schools, shared parish picnics, a program of bi-annual pancake breakfasts, and many more.

Over the years, besides friendships and projects, jobs and job training became a valuable outgrowth of the sharing program.

Finally in the 1990s, one member of St. Anne's had his company take on a full sponsorship of St. Cyril School. This included regular volunteer hours of his working staff, great and expansive technological help and resources, and outright financial support.

The culmination of the sharing project was a special expression of the Gospel for both parishes.

The Call

During my teaching years, I had a unique experience that I want to share. It fit into a pattern of The Call, God's invitation that is so much part of all our journeys.

The more I experience the Christian journey, the more I feel that there is only one call in our lives. We have special occasions when it is more apparent and more engulfing. We develop and it becomes clearer according to our spiritual growth that enables us to handle its ever increasing demands.

To understand my call to the Carmelites, you have to understand St. Laurence parish in Chicago in the 1950s. I was seventh child of Irish immigrants, Cornelius and Bridget O'Sullivan, who arrived in the United States on July 4, 1923, with two infant children. Six of the eight of us were born in St. Laurence parish.

St. Laurence was the anchor and center of a supportive and life-giving culture especially if you were Catholic and more so if you were Irish. The lynch pin was Monsignor Patrick McGuire. For me he was more a symbol than a reality. He was the one who put everything in order and let us feel comfortable and proud in our place.

A few years before I was born in the final days of Prohibition, my father spent six months in the hospital from a bad brew of alcohol he made in our basement. Monsignor McGuire, through the parish programs, helped the family in the Depression and with this extended medical crisis for my father.

He earned the undying and unquestioning loyalty of my mother for this help and concern in one her darkest times.

My mother was very involved in the parish. She was loved in the neighborhood as a gentle soul with a spectacular sense of humor. She never missed a PTA meeting or the other events or performances for all eight of her kids. If someone needed something from the parish, very often they came to Mrs. O'Sullivan to help open the process. She loved the parish with a passion. The same was the case for Mt. Carmel High School and Loretto High School where all her sons and daughters attended high school.

My father never made a meeting but did come to see me play football. On the other hand, he had a passion for justice and for the working man and unions that penetrated my mind and heart.

These two patterns of my parents played a powerful role in my life.

For my family the idea of being a priest was viewed as an exclusive and privileged position. The only thing higher for me as a young boy would be to be the quarterback at Notre Dame.

I had a troubled ride at St. Laurence School. I flunked second grade. I was in the dummy group in third grade and made a little progress in fourth grade. However, it did not seem to bother me much. In fifth grade there was a big change. I was the smartest kid in the class.

Later on, I learned that it all had to do with my mother worrying about my two brothers in the war. When the war ended, I was going into fifth grade.

Three events in my fourth grade help capture the signs of the times at St. Laurence. They also show a hidden desire to break loose from the subtle captivity of the mixed bag of culture and religion that I would later call my "South Side Irish Tribal Customs." This urge to go beyond would ultimately attract me to the Carmelites rather than the diocesan priesthood.

In the fall of 1944 we prayed three Hail Marys every day for Notre Dame. The week that they played Army we prayed especially hard. They lost 59-0. That was the beginning of the end to the St. Laurence worldview for me. What kind of God would let Notre Dame lose like that?

Then one Sunday I had the beginning of my Vatican II journey. The entire school attended the nine AM Mass. The good Sister sat behind us to insure our behavior. We had to keep silence and keep in order especially at Communion time.

This particular Sunday I got into an unthinkable predicament! I received two hosts at Communion time. In my eyes, the dilemma was beyond life and death. If I swallowed the second host I believed the floor would open up and I would go straight to hell. If I took it out of my mouth…that just was not an option!

So I tried to keep one host on the side of my mouth with the intention of bringing it to the Monsignor after the Mass. No such luck. It melted away. However, the trip to hell somehow seemed delayed. The floor stayed in place much to my relief.

Right after the Mass I raced to the sacristy to explain everything to the Monsignor. He was kind and gentle with me. "Oh don't worry about it, my son. That's not your fault."

My outward reaction was equally appropriate. "Thank you, Monsignor." Inside, however, I was saying this whole system is crazy. I almost died and went to hell and he says "don't worry about it." That gave me a twenty year head start on Vatican II to begin to break loose of the closed and comfortable world of St. Laurence.

Finally, there was the triangular ruler. Our teacher, Sister Julia Ann, used this ruler on our knuckles if she determined it was necessary for continued order in the universe. It happened far too often for me and a friend, Jack Hennelly.

One day we were in the school during lunch time and our classroom was open. We spotted the ruler out in the open on her desk. We both looked at each other and said "Yes!!" We took it out in the alley and broke it into small pieces and hid them deep in the garbage can. We never got caught. Here again was a new opening in the closed world of St. Laurence.

When I was in seventh grade, the Carmelite vocation director came to give the pitch to join the Carmelites. I had a sense of adventure of entering a new world but still maintaining the comfort and beauty of St. Laurence. I signed up.

Two weeks later I regretted it when I thought about my playing football at Mt. Carmel High and besides, the young ladies were getting more interesting each passing day.

I decided to go to Mt. Carmel, played quarterback on the third consecutive City Championship team and was the quarterback and co-captain of the first Mt. Carmel team to lose the city championship in four years in my senior year.

After the devastating loss, from late November to early February, I was floundering. My life seemed empty for the first time. I received scholarship offers from many colleges and letters of inquiry from even more colleges but nothing excited me. Then one day, in the midst of this funk, I was walking home from school. I was in front of St. Laurence church. I said to myself, "I'm going to go to Niagara." (The Carmelite seminary at Niagara Falls). Since seventh grade, five years earlier, the desire to join the Carmelites and go to Niagara had been deep but hidden background music to my total commitment to football and responding to the young ladies in an age appropriate way.

There were no bells and whistles. The angels stayed in heaven and kept the music in heaven. I just began to slowly feel at peace. Over the next week I just grew more convinced and, finally, I went to talk to my parish priest, Fr. Jim Brazil, who guided me through the next several months of transition.

Looking back over many years and even decades, I see that decision as the most important choice in my life. On the surface, I was choosing a college and a vague sense of a way of life. Down deep, I was saying "yes" to God but it would take a good while to become clear. What was important was the decision, not the clarity, because God has *"been there all along."*

The Call: II

While I look back at the moment in front of St. Laurence as my foundational "call" by God, there have been countless experiences where this has been renewed.

But I have had few experiences where I openly considered a different option. One of these was in what I call my midlife crisis in the early 1970s. Much more common for me has been a slide into mediocrity and lack of focus.

Looking back, the entire period of my "Fifteen Minutes of Fame" was a slow slide into confusion in how I was seeking the Lord. Part of it was my agenda, my own self-absorption. This may have been normal at this age but part of it was being overwhelmed by the depth of the racial problem.

As head of the Civil Rights Committee, I had continual encounters with situations of abuse, violence, and just crude racism. For the Jackson Park Hospital case alone, I interviewed over sixty individuals who were mistreated by the hospital and experienced great pain and humiliation. I had dozens of encounters with people who felt physically abused by the police. Then there was the continual gang violence and many incidents of domestic violence. The net result was that I was an angry young man.

The switch to the classroom was the beginning of a process of healing. One event crystallizes the movement to healing. This happened on a day late in May 1973, on the last day of my final course for a masters degree in urban studies at Loyola University. This degree was necessary for my position as principal.

I got up at 5 AM to work on the conclusion of my last term paper. I taught classes in the morning and then headed to Loyola to finish my paper and attend the final class. I returned home at 9 PM ready to relax and watch the White Sox. I was exhausted but relieved.

I was home alone that night. All of a sudden, I heard a lot of noise and racket in the passage way between the rectory and the church. I looked out the window and saw a group of youngsters howling, laughing and throwing rocks. I told them to go away. Usually this was sufficient because I was well known and respected by most of the kids in the neighborhood. This time was different. They started calling me names. Despite repeated demands, it continued. So I was driven to do something I hated to do. I reluctantly called the police for whom I held deep resentment. They arrived quickly and the kids fled.

The officers rang the bell. I answered. They told me there was a dead man in the passage way between the rectory and the church. I told them they were crazy. So we went out to the passageway. As we approached the gate, the only light came from the streetlight. It was spooky. We saw a man, half in the shadow and half in the dim light, sitting against the wall at the top of the stairs leading to the parish meeting room. It appeared as if his brains were pouring out of his head and down over his face. It was a very disturbing and frightening scene.

As I opened the gate and we approached the man, he began to move. As we got closer the picture got clearer. At his feet was a broken glass jar. On his face were the remnants of the jar, strawberry jam.

He said, "What time is the meeting?" He was drunk and late for the AA meeting six hours earlier. The kids were throwing rocks and apparently strawberry jam at him while he was trying sleep it off.

I was really angry at the man. I had had enough for the day. Meanwhile, one of the policemen went back to the squad car and returned with gloves and a towel. He began to wipe his face.

At that moment I had a singular experience, never again repeated in my life. I had an incredibly beautiful and gentle vision of an image of Jesus. It touched my soul profoundly. There was not a lot of emotion but a deep and strong sense of presence. I cannot say whether it was quick or slow only deep and real.

Later, when I reflected on it, the most curious element was that I could not determine whether Jesus was in the man or in the officer wiping his face.

The experience signaled the beginning of a long term process of healing and reconciliation that I experienced over the next several years.

The first thing to change was my attitude toward the police. I became more accepting of their job and began to understand how difficult it was. Then I had a gradual growth in patience with others and especially with myself. My understanding of the depth of the parable of the weeds and the wheat grew slowly. I experienced this steady transformation but over the years realized it was connected to that profound experience.

Many years later I ran across a saying from Julian of Norwich, a mystic of the Middle Ages. It hit the nail on the head for me. She said, "First comes the fall, then the conversion. In both we find the mercy of God." This was just another manifestation that God has *"been there all along."*

The Call: III

Another significant dimension of the "call" happened when I was at Whitefriars Hall. This was in January of 1994. I was in charge of the seminary house for the Carmelites in Washington, D.C. I had made a commitment of six years and was in my fourth year. Once again, I felt some unrest. I acknowledged it as a desire to work with the poor.

One day I had a chance to talk with Fr. Ernie Larkin who had been a major spiritual guide most of my life. He gave me a simple formula: simply go to prayer and be quiet and listen. Do not bring up concerns or issues. I did and God spoke.

I cannot remember how many days or weeks I prayed following Ernie's guidance, but soon enough something quite unexpected surfaced in my heart. I realized that I never really mourned the enormous uprooting after twenty-five years in Chicago.

I let myself hurt and mourn and cry. I remember the tears which were not common in my life. Again, the time frame escapes me. Whether it was days or weeks, I do not know. What I do remember clearly was that my provincial, Quinn Conners, came to my door with a request to discuss an issue with me.

Previously, I had shared with Quinn that I had a desire to return to work with the poor which I now understood was more specifically that I return to Chicago. Quinn asked me if I would consider going to St. Raphael parish in Los Angeles.

I know that if I had not gone through that experience of mourning my departure from Chicago, I would have come up with a truckload of reasons why I could not go to LA.

Indeed, I like to say everybody remembers the day, some months later, when I arrived in LA. I passed O.J. Simpson in the air as he was going to Chicago on the infamous Sunday evening when his wife was murdered. I call it a straight player trade: me for OJ, no cash involved.

I am now in my nineteenth year at St. Raphael in South Central Los Angeles. It has truly been a call from God.

The Call: IV

Another area of "The Call" has been the challenging and often difficult but eventually beautiful reality of the celibate life. I would like to share some observations about celibacy and then some of my personal journey.

Despite all the attention it gets, celibacy is not understood with much clarity in today's Church. Most see it much more as a necessary discipline than as a life-giving mystery. Ninety-five percent of the conversation is about whether it is necessary or not. I hear very little about celibacy as an important element in our search for God.

I heard one wise priest give this practical analysis of celibacy for today's clergy: for some, it makes them saints, for some, it makes them liars, for many, it makes them bachelors.

What is seldom said about celibacy is that it is you have to grow into it. It offers new challenges at the different stages of one's life.

We need to understand that in the final analysis, celibacy is not about our sexuality but about our spirituality. It is the spiritual component that places the celibate experience at the center of the search for God.

Having said that, I can testify that celibacy is somewhat easier at 75 than at 35!

My generation was poorly prepared to live a celibate life. I use the following markers to define my generation as a Carmelite. My generation includes a seven year period, 1959 to 1965, with three classes ahead and three classes behind the year of my class. There were 100 men ordained as Carmelite priests in these years from 1954-1965. Fifty-two left the priesthood. Several more can be described as walking wounded.

While this is a very small sample, I think it is typical of our Church's experience in the United States during these volatile years.

Our generation left the seminary to encounter a very powerful set of movements in society.

In short order we met the sexual revolution in the unstable, first days of this radical change. Then, we walked into the social, political, and cultural changes we call the sixties with Vietnam, civil rights, and the murders of our leaders. In the Church the phenomenon of Vatican II contributed to the extreme youthful enthusiasm and the uprooting and shattering of boundaries, expectations, and, often, common sense constraints.

To show the depth of the time warp we found ourselves in, I point out two 19th century, if not 18th century, practices of our seminary days which were geared to protect our celibate state of life. We had always to go out with a partner and, for a reason known to very few, we had to wear a hat. These practices were not far removed from the suggestion of the nuns in our high school days that we bring a telephone book if one of the girls had to sit on a boy's lap in a crowded car. Strange as it may seem, falling in love helped me to find my bearings as a loving celibate in my journey through these troubling times.

Three times, as a priest, in different eras of my life, I fell in love. Each time it was a marvelous, exciting, frightening, confusing, and ultimately, rich and rewarding experience. I had to address who I was and how I wanted to live. I had to question my commitment all over again.

Each time, I was blessed with a woman of maturity and wisdom who was patient and kind, understanding, and in the end, supportive of my choice. The road from romance to reality is quite a trip.

Each adventure was a great story but I will only say that I am much more committed today to my celibate calling than before these experiences. My eyes are open to the choices that are involved. I have been blessed through these encounters with love and life.

In 1990, preparing to lead the Carmelite seminary in DC, I took a course on spirituality and human development. For my paper, I wrote on celibacy as part of the formation program for seminarians. I concluded the paper with these thoughts which are even more appropriate today when we live with the fallout of the child sexual abuse scandal.

"Upon reflection, I cannot recall the last positive conversation I have heard or been involved in about celibacy. Much more often than not, it is viewed as an embarrassment, as necessary baggage for a life of ministry and the clerical state.

"In all my years as a Carmelite, I do not remember ever hearing an enthusiastic declaration about our mutual celibate commitment as a major gift in our life. There is always talk of community but celibacy never gets on the floor of the assembly or the issue at the table of conversation.

"Taking the time to study, reflect, and pray about this paper, I have come to a new awareness of the gift and challenge of celibacy, a new appreciation of its wonder. It has to be central to any spiritual renewal we seek. It can no longer be our well-kept secret.

"At the heart of the celibate life is the call to love as tender and compassionate men. At the heart of the celibate life is a call to pray, to encounter the God we seek. At the heart of the celibate life is the call to witness to a new way of being in the world, a way that will hear the cry of the poor and work for justice. At the heart of the celibate life is a call to be truly human and free to cherish the gift of each person in new freedom.

"The obvious challenge is to integrate all the far-ranging demands of human development with a deeply rooted spirituality to journey the long road to the celibate ideal. It is, indeed, far from an embarrassment but a powerful and wondrous beckoning of the Lord."

5

A Year Under the Golden Dome

In November 1974, I was invited out to dinner by a good friend, Father Jim Gillen. Fr. Gillen was a member of our provincial council and in charge of our high schools. He asked me to consider becoming the principal of our high school in Los Angeles. I agreed to go out there for a visit and look at the situation.

After a visit that included my first view of palm trees, I asked if I could have one more year at St. Cyril to make a smooth transition to a new administration. The provincial agreed, but then decided six months later to close the Los Angeles school.

I thought I was then free to continue at St. Cyril but Fr. Paul, our provincial, had other plans. Our dialogue soon became tense and basically deadlocked. Jim Gillen came to the rescue. He suggested that I take a year at the University of Notre Dame in the religious leaders program led by Monsignor Jack Egan.

I arrived at the South Bend campus, 80 miles from Chicago, right before Christmas in 1976 after a painful farewell at St. Clara-St. Cyril. My residence was Brownson Hall, literally right under the Golden Dome. The year of studies, reflection, prayer, and relaxation was one of the truly great events in my life. I spent a minimal amount of time in the religious leaders program which was mostly for ex-provincials and superiors of religious orders. I invested myself in the pursuit of a masters degree in pastoral theology.

Several things happened in my year of study and prayer at Notre Dame. First of all, the coach reluctantly gave in after a historic loss to Mississippi and started to play a quarterback he did not like. His name was Montana and they celebrated New Year's Day as national champs.

A second thing of interest was that I began to help out celebrating Mass on Sundays at parishes in Edwardsburg and Cassapolis, Michigan, about twenty-five miles from the campus. I found out some really wonderful things in the process. I could enjoy being a priest. I learned a great deal about liturgy. I realized that I was a good homilist and a very good storyteller in the pulpit. I also was introduced into the Catholic "don't ask, don't tell" game about birth control. This weekend pastoral experience proved to be a very helpful bridge from my Woodlawn community organizer days to my post-ND assignment in a white suburb.

One of the significant things that transpired during the year is that I had a meaningful encounter with the theology of Vatican II. One year is a short time for such a sublime task but it was a glorious beginning of the quest of a lifetime.

A special gift of my academic stay was the opportunity to reflect on my Woodlawn experience. A truly interesting development happened to me as I began to get deeper into the issues. Two important men from my youth at St. Laurence came into my consciousness. They were Monsignor McGuire and Dr. Harmon, our family doctor and my hero. I began to see my Woodlawn journey as a movement from Monsignor McGuire's worldview to Dr. Harmon's approach.

Dr. Harmon was an important person, deeply loved by all my family and much of the neighborhood. He was a local doctor who lived on the next block. He seemed always to be there when we needed him. He had a reputation for gruffness but was always kind and gentle when things became difficult, or when deep understanding was needed. Dr. Harmon always seemed to be there. I heard stories of how he did not charge those folks who were out of work. He seemed to constantly have a cigar and I began to love the smell of cigars and eventually imitated my hero for far too long in my later life.

One incident is ingrained in my memory. My sister Therese was about five years old and riding on the back of my brother Connie's two-wheel bike. She caught her ankle in the spokes of the wheel. It was a horrible sight for me as an eight-year-old child. Blood seemed to be everywhere. I was sure she was going to die. Connie picked her up and ran down the street to Dr. Harmon's house. He was at dinner. He placed her on the front room's couch and treated the wound in no time. For me, it was as if I had just seen God in action.

I recall a Sunday afternoon when Dr. Harmon became the subject of a major theological conversation for all the family. That morning the Monsignor preached the common pre-Vatican II belief that anyone who was not Catholic was going to hell. Dr. Harmon was not only not Catholic, he was not sure what he believed about God.

His faith, or lack of faith, created a conflict for all of the family. Even as a young boy, I could see the dilemma. Our view of the world was directed and guided by commitment to the Monsignor as the guardian of God's truth. On the other hand, Dr. Harmon was the concrete human expression of everything we believed was good and loving. No one was comparable to him, especially the Monsignor, whom my father disliked because he was rich, took most of

Lent as a vacation in Florida, and drove a Cadillac.

Later when I came to reflect on my ministry at St. Clara and St. Cyril, I saw it as the switch from the *Chicago Plan* of trying to bring the people into the Church to the Servant Church model as a switch from the Monsignor model to the Doctor Harmon model. The Monsignor model, deeply embedded through my seminary training, had given me a confident fix on reality. It was neat, comfortable, and under my control because as a priest, I was the chosen instrument of God and his messenger. My years in Woodlawn shattered that view and undermined my role which I facetiously labeled as passing on the "South Side Irish Tribal Customs." My switch was to the Dr. Harmon model where I would serve God's suffering people. I would reach out and heal. I would change the system.

But the deeper I went into my studies and reflection, the more clarity faded from me. Confusion let me see that I was not going to find the answer in either the Monsignor or the Doctor models. My clear black and white handle on reality was going grey. The "either/or" was moving to the much more challenging "both/and." The central issue I came to see was my idea of God. I needed to trade in my old understanding for one expressed by Vatican II. This was at the heart of my marvelous experience at Notre Dame in the special year of 1977.

Slowly I began to realize that I had shortchanged the image of the Monsignor and the "South Side Irish Tribal Customs." There was a sense of prayer, majesty, beauty, grandeur, and wisdom all wrapped up in the belittled "South Side Irish Tribal Customs." There were riches in what had been put aside by my youthful impatience. Once again, I began to see how the parable of the weeds and the wheat expresses the depth of reality in a consequential way.

On the other hand, I had bought into the Servant Church model 100 percent that I now was identifying with the Doctor model. It also came in for critique. My experience showed me that in spite of the heroic stance in the footsteps of Dr. Harmon, progress was less substantial and the problems were clearly much more deep-rooted than I ever dreamed. Built into the Doctor's approach was a gradual temptation to see oneself bringing in the Kingdom. The messianic urges were always just beneath the surface, if not out in the open.

Liberating Confusion

I had made a commitment to immerse myself into life and let the experience talk to me. The Augustinian writer Gregory Baum[9] initiated a dramatic breakthrough for me. He gave me a clearer and deeper language to let the experience reach me. Baum talked of an insider God, as the deepest expression of what is most authentically human **but always more**. He cast away the outsider God who was removed from life, outside the human struggle and, more often than not, a stern judge.

Baum pointed out that Vatican II's *Pastoral Constitution on the Church in the Modern World* points to the redemptive involvement of God with all humankind. A person engaged in dialogue with others hears a voice in one's conscience that goes beyond one's own thoughts to God speaking and calling. The document says a new human is emerging in which the human person is primarily defined by one's responsibility to one's brothers and sisters and to history. Baum pointed out that, in this view, the Gospel becomes the Good News about human life. This leads to a new sense of brotherhood and sisterhood that goes beyond the Church to all others. Likewise, this means that truth comes from many sources far beyond the Church.

This experience of brothers and sisters is one of the sources of truth that has led to new insights. The Good News is present to human life. God is redeeming all of human history. One of the more delightful consequences of this insight was that Dr. Harmon probably had a grand welcome from my mother when he got past St. Peter.

> "Wherever people are, something happens. People are not left to their destructive inclinations and awful games they play; a transcendent power is operative in their lives, calling them to self-knowledge and freeing them to leave their destructive past behind and enter into new life. God is present to history in the growth and reconciliation of man."[11]

Baum's insight about God as the deepest expression of human reality drove me to ponder and pray about how I could integrate the approaches to ministry symbolized by the Monsignor and the Doctor.

As I worked for the master's degree in pastoral theology, this question became clearer: where do I find God in my service to the Gospel? How does preaching and living the Good News become central to this search for God?

There were no easy answers but I found myself being pushed toward a liberating confusion. It was great to know that I did not have all the answers. At the same time, my search for God called me to a deeper love for prayer and spirituality, as equally important components with action and service, as part of my ministry to the Gospel.

In one of the classes we talked about the mission of the Church in light of these new theological developments. We were given a question: Is the mission of the Church to baptize the slaves or to work for their freedom? This opened up a wide area of the relation of evangelization and development. Is the Church missionary? Is the Church servant? Is the Church advocate for the poor? Is the Church educator? Is the Church an agent of social change?

Of course she is all of these roles. The question that permeated my study and reflection was: How do the Church and her ministers balance all of these? These questions energized my time at Notre Dame. I did not know if I would integrate the Monsignor and the Doctor but the effort to do so was both enlightening and life-giving. I was beginning to learn that the grace is in the struggle and not in the accomplishment.

Wrapping It Up

Notre Dame was and is a national center for much of the intellectual and pastoral life of the Church in the United States. The university hosted both programs and national gatherings of people working in urban ministry and in liturgy. Many of these groups had contrasting styles and visions. There was little interchange and, more than a fair share of disdain, particularly on the part of the urban ministry crowd. The latter were the Dr. Harmon program on steroids. The liturgists just seemed different and unconnected to me.

At one session of the national urban ministers something unusual happened. A prominent nun gave a talk. During her presentation she led the entire group in a session of centering prayer. This was a significant step in leading all groups to a more overt spirituality, and eventually, to an integration that would reduce the barriers between the "in the street" urban ministry folks and the "in the church" liturgy folks. I was not the only one trying to bring Monsignor McGuire and Dr. Harmon together.

As the year drew to a close, I asked myself the question that is on the mind of most forty-two year olds. What am I going to be when I grow up? I came up with a clear answer. I wanted to be a Carmelite. I did not, however, have a clear and concrete idea of what it meant to be a Carmelite. Nevertheless, the decision would be fruitful and productive for the rest of my life.

During the year, I had several conversations with Monsignor Jack Egan. He had a marvelous talent as both a genuine listener and a gentle guide. As the year drew to a close, I told Jack that I had a desire to explain to people what the Black community in Woodlawn was experiencing and how it is connected to the larger mission of the Church and our search for the Gospel. Jack had an immediate suggestion. He said I needed to learn to work with White folks. He had an idea and he would get back to me.

A week later, I had another of those dinners that was going to impact my immediate future. I was with Fr. Leo Mahon, a famous Chicago priest who was pastor of St. Victor parish in Calumet City, Illinois, a Chicago suburb.

Leo was one of the most creative and exciting pastors in the archdiocese, if not the entire country. He had spent ten years in Panama as a missionary for the archdiocese. While there, he started the program of Bible study that led to the base community movement in all of Latin America. This was a movement where people joined in small groups to regularly reflect and pray on the Bible and set actions in play to better their lives at all levels. He was now trying to bring the same Bible-based conversion experience to a suburban parish outside of Chicago.

Jack had recommended me to Leo and Leo was happy to have me.

A few days later Leo called and said there was a problem. My reputation had preceded me. His staff voted not to accept me. They felt I would be too harsh with the people and would bring more problems than they needed.

Leo set up a meeting with the staff. Apparently, I was more caring in person than my press clippings had portrayed me. I won them over and began what was planned to be a year-and-a-half program.

6

ST. VICTOR'S

I arrived at St. Victor on December 1, 1978, with the intention of spending the next year and half as an associate pastor. At the time of my arrival it was a lower middleclass neighborhood. It was a predominantly white, blue-collar population.

Leo Mahon, the pastor, chose this parish because its demographics contrasted to his work among the poor in Panama. He wanted to show that his pastoral vision transcended demographics and would work anywhere.

The pastoral plan for St. Victor was simple, forthright, and powerful. People were called to conversion through an encounter with the Word of God and the Sacraments. This goal permeated all ministries of the parish but there were two unique expressions of it.

The first was the Jubilee Weekend. This was a weekend retreat held in the former convent that had been transformed into a parish retreat center. Parishioners were recruited to experience this initial call to conversion. Members of the parish were trained to organize the event and give most of the talks.

The second program was a follow up to the Jubilee Weekend. This was called the College of Ministry. The parishioners were prepared for various ministries and given ongoing formation that kept the challenge of the Gospel always beyond their present stage of development. Here again the parishioners handled the majority of the presentations.

The liturgy was an integral part of the ongoing formation. It was lively, solemn, and joyful with enough variety to meet the needs of a diverse community. Choirs tapped into a variety of musical styles. Full participation was the norm and the reality.

Through these elements of ministry and the activities of the parish programs, the message of the Word and the Sacrament became a pulsating invitation to meet Christ. In 1978, very few parishes had this kind of clarity, organization, or resources for such a pastoral plan. I was privileged to become part of it.

My Beginning

My transition to St. Victor's was rather smooth. However, one surprise for me was the increase in both the quantity and quality of my prayer. I suppose the move set me free from the pressure of papers and tests at Notre Dame. Another factor was the desire to ponder the many insights I gathered in my studies. I had little pressure from the schedule at the parish in the beginning. This kind of freedom was new to me. The call to prayer filled the void.

My pastoral goals were simple. I needed to learn how to minister in a White parish. I needed to learn how to become comfortable with myself as a priest and as a cleric. I had a good beginning on my weekend work at the Michigan parishes but this was now a full time job in a high powered pastoral situation.

On a personal level, I had several goals. First and foremost, I wanted to grow. This goal was founded on Lonergan's transcendental precepts that I learned in a course at Notre Dame: be attentive, be intelligent, be reasonable, be responsible, and be loving. This vision was extremely attractive to me. It fit my desire to plunge into life, into the real. It offered a spirituality that connected with my desire to work for justice and peace, another new term I had just learned at the South Bend campus.

Until this time my pattern had been to work hard and then fill the rest of the day with fluff time: news, sports, and drinking. I wanted to change this. It would become a thirty-year project.

A second goal was to get in touch with my feelings and, in particular, areas where I would share more deeply and honestly with others.

A third goal was to learn to work as a member of a group. During my time as a minister, I had been in charge.

In my second week at St. Victor I had a surprising thought, totally disconnected from getting adjusted to the new parish setting. I wanted to start a small group of Carmelites who would be serious about prayer and lifestyle as well as ministry.

Leo

My first task was to get to know Leo and learn how to work with him. He was a character bigger than life. Leo was in constant demand for consultation about his experience and his pastoral plan. Many people were studying the beginning of the base communities in Latin America. On this topic Leo was a primary resource. Others were interested in the application of the vision to a White, middleclass setting. The result was a constant flow of visitors trying to get on Leo's schedule.

Leo was also the critical analyst of developments in the archdiocese and the purveyor of a fair amount of clerical gossip among Chicago priests. Father Andrew Greely, the famous author, sociologist and critic, had Leo as his hero from his seminary days. They were in touch regularly. Andy was a major source of information for Leo. The activities of the not-so-beloved Cardinal Cody were at the heart of these conversations and speculations. It seemed as if there was at least one, new, juicy item every day.

I was startled to learn how respectful Leo was of his bishop despite the tremendous difference in their outlooks on the Church and reality.

I remember sitting in on a session with Leo and some bright young priests of the archdiocese. They wanted to pick his brain about a better way to reach young adults. Theology on Tap, which became a long standing national program, was the consequence of that conversation.

One idea that I gained from Leo was the scriptural reflection at the beginning of the staff meeting each Monday morning. After reading the coming Sunday's Gospel, we shared as a staff how that Gospel passage could take flesh in the pastoral plan and activities of the parish. I have carried that practice wherever I have been for the last thirty-five years.

Leo had a young associate by the name of Bill Stenzel. He was a high-powered and talented man who was studying to be an alcoholic counselor at the time of my arrival. He made a great contribution to many families as a pioneer in that field. My sister Peggy, among many, was truly blessed through his dynamic workshops. While raising twelve children she had to deal with husband who never recovered. All the while she maintained a sense of peace as she flowed from one crisis to the next. She and my sister Therese are my heroes.

Parish Priest

I found it delightful to learn how to do the ordinary stuff of a parish priest. The routine of funerals, weddings, and baptisms were new to me but I enjoyed being present to the people.

I soon became aware of how much ego went into my preaching. I was good, and at times very good. I learned how easy it is to slip away from preaching the Gospel of Jesus to the Gospel of Tracy. The choice between being popular or being faithful is a temptation every preacher faces. Competition between good preachers just heightens this call to be faithful to the Gospel.

I remember especially fondly my role as the chaplain of the Italian Catholic Federation. The St. Joseph's Table is a long way from the streets of Woodlawn!

One of the clear tests I had was to avoid getting sucked into the different "in groups" of the parish. The fact that I played football at Mt. Carmel was a held in high esteem. The fact that I ministered for twelve years in the Black community was just the opposite. I had to tread a careful path to maintain my integrity on the race issue. As I gained support among the people, I was able to talk and preach about the race issue and call forth a Gospel vision in a challenging and realistic way. I was slowly developing the skill to call forth people without putting them down, a subtle but essential art for one who wants to proclaim the message of Jesus.

At this time I read an article that has stayed with me to this day. The article said that when we preach the Gospel there has to be both balance and tension between a message of comfort and a message of challenge. The Gospel preaching has to address the struggle and confusion of people with words of hope and support. At the same time it always has to call for more. It must maintain a challenging dimension.

Later on, I would verbalize this part of the Gospel challenge by saying we are into mortgages and God is into pilgrimages.

I encountered conflict in the concrete, as different groups in the parish wanted me to buy into their way of seeing things. This, I soon learned, was the great temptation at St. Victor. They were all so proud of their great activities and of the parish as a whole, that any criticism was a threat and easily rejected. It was hard here, as well as everywhere else, to preach the Gospel of Jesus without diluting it. The components of comfort and challenge are held in balance with great difficulty and demand maturity and wisdom.

In this struggle I was having an intuitive response to something I would see more clearly later on. The Gospel needs to be open and sensitive to the culture but we must realize that no culture contains the full integrity of the Gospel. The Gospel always stands as a critic of the culture. This fine equilibrium and tension is at the heart of pastoral ministry.

The Gift of Friendship

During this time there was another person who became important in my life. Fr. Dennis Geaney was an Augustinian priest who worked in the pastoral ministry program at the Catholic Theological Union. He had a great interest in Leo's program. We had known each other before but at this time we became close friends.

We loved to talk about Leo. We both were excited by his vision and imagination. We also were critical. We agreed that Leo missed the sixties. He was not sensitive to the race issue and his life style was far from simple. We called him our "Magnificent Enigma."

Dennis was twenty years older than I and we shared many struggles and blessings along the way as voices of social concern within our respective Orders. When I left St. Victor, Dennis took my place. We stayed in close touch over the years. One of the more poignant moments in my life occurred fourteen years later when I was in Washington, D.C. Dennis called me to say goodbye less than a half hour before he died.

The Carmelite Thing

My time at St. Victor proved to be a rich learning experience. However, no particular parish program or ministry grabbed me. The Lord was calling me in a different direction. The idea of starting a Carmelite house that would focus on a combination of prayer and reflection on how to best serve the poor kept percolating in my mind and heart.

After several months I talked with Leo about it and he strongly encouraged me to take the leadership role and make it happen. While the idea and the desire were getting steadily stronger, the practicalities of how to do it were extremely vague.

During this time I arranged a workshop on serving the poor and justice and peace for my Carmelite brothers. The topic generated some enthusiasm for the social justice issues. However, it sparked little interest for my idea, which was anything but concrete and clear.

Two Public Statements to the Carmelite Province

In the summer of 1977 I had a meeting with the Carmelite provincial, Fr. Paul Hoban, and his council. I wanted to share a deep concern. I felt that the commitment to prayer and a call to deeper spirituality that Paul was encouraging were good. However, a critical component was missing. The style of prayer was privatized and devoid of openness to the social and justice elements of the Gospel message. The provincial and his council suggested that I write up my concerns and share them with the members of the province. I did.

In May 1978, in anticipation of the upcoming Chapter to elect new officials and set new directions for the province, I wrote a lengthy proposal to establish a house of refection and prayer at St. Clara's priory in Woodlawn. The goal would be a community both serious about prayer and creative about ways to better serve the poor.

I believe these documents led to my election as a member of the new provincial council made up of four councilors in June 1978. My election caused my premature departure from St. Victor after only six months and my move back to Woodlawn to establish the proposed house of prayer.

Reflection

Many positive things that came from my short stay at St. Victor:

I definitely was praying more, and more consistently.

The pastoral vision drew me into a greater love of the Scriptures. I learned to place the Word of God at the center of my ministry.

I learned how to be a better celebrant and leader at the liturgy and developed a more profound grasp of liturgy as an event of the community.

I began to learn to take people where they are and call them forth to a new space.

I learned to see that the parish community is the primary evangelizing instrument in the neighborhood. The priest is to work at creating the community by Word and Sacrament.

I learned that I still was called to some form of ministry which involved working more closely with the poor. How his would take place was still in the gestation process.

On the negative side I have a few quotes from my journal that I would like to share:

"I am determined to drink less. I have begun a program where I will drink only three days a week."

"I have been thinking how I am programmed by the schedule. It seems that habit or whatever makes study at night not too common. This has something to do with drinking also. When I have a few drinks any kind of serious study or intense involvement is very unlikely. I ought to take these things out in the open and examine the price I pay for them and see if I want to change the way I use my time between 5 and 11 PM. This is definitely my least productive time span."

Of course, I was clueless about the pain implicit in the last two comments. But here again I would learn that in the upcoming darkness God has *been there all along.*

7

The Justice Perspective

The provincial chapter in June 1978, was a changing of the guard. Fr. John Malley, the new provincial, was an intelligent, sensitive and practical man. He had an extraordinary gift for engaging with people. There was not a receptionist, cook, or maintenance man in any house of the province that John could not name and tell at least the headlines of their story. He was truly exceptional. He proved to be a great support for me personally. One of my important jobs was to help John see the importance of justice and peace in our Carmelite mission. At the beginning he did not see it.

A second person who proved to be very helpful was Fr. Joel Schevers. Joel was the first councilor and an intelligent, well-prepared participant in our bi-monthly meetings. Joel took me under his wing and encouraged my pioneering work in justice and peace. Joel was 20 years older than I and he became a wonderful model of aging gracefully while slowly diminishing involvement in ministry.

John interpreted my election as acceptance for my proposal of a house of reflection and prayer at St Clara. He gave me full support, even allowing me to recruit among the members.

While the surprise and thrill of these events began to subside, I moved into St. Clara. Now, however, I had a problem. First of all no one volunteered to come even though I received strong encouragement from many. Secondly I still had not developed a realistic agenda.

Three Powerful Experiences

John asked me to attend a workshop in Cleveland held for all religious in the US. It was on prayer, simplicity of lifestyle, and justice and peace. More than 3,000 religious gathered. One dynamite speaker after another filled me with fiery enthusiasm and gave me some good connections and a load of resources.

After the conference I went from Cleveland to Washington, D.C., to visit one of our saintly Carmelites, Fr. Peter Hinde. Peter had been in the missions in Peru for several years. Returning to the States, he began a new and creative ministry. He established Tabor House as a gathering place for people, information, and programs for returning missionaries. He and his co-founder, Sr. Betty Campbell, a Mercy nun, modeled a life of deep prayer and gospel simplicity.

At this time many of these men and women were coming back from their mission assignments. Tabor House helped them and others understand the incredible impact, mostly destructive, of US policies and other political and economic realities on the lives of the poor in Latin America.

I spent a week of immersion with Peter and Betty. I began to grasp the depth of the problem which was clear to Peter, Betty, and the handful of missionaries that they had in residence that week. The week began a lifetime of learning from Peter and Betty who live the gospel with the same intensity and wonder today at the age of 91.

After I returned to Chicago I attended a week long workshop on the spirituality of John of the Cross presented by Fr. Ernie Larkin. Ernie had taught us John of the Cross and Teresa of Avila in the seminary fifteen years earlier. He now had re-experienced the great Carmelite Doctors of the Church in light of Vatican II. He brought them to life for me in an entirely new way. Here again, the workshop gave me a giant step on the path out of ignorance about my Carmelite heritage.

When I returned to St. Clara, after almost a month away, I finally had a sense of where to begin my cherished project. Study and prayer were the order of the day. The summer experiences had given me a sense of direction.

Search for Members

After about six weeks of study and prayer, I began to recruit. Since I had no Carmelite volunteers at this time, I began to reach out to the priests, nuns and lay ministers I had known from my earlier days in Woodlawn. I held a series of luncheons at the priory. In all, about 30 people attended. Most were curious because of my reputation but they found the concept beyond their idea of parish ministry. I had no recruits, not even a serious nibble.

Then one day I got a phone call from a fellow I had met briefly some years before. He was Dan Daley, a resigned priest. After a series of conversations Dan and his wife Shelia agreed to a luncheon date. This led to another long session where we planned a series of weekly meetings to share ideas and information on this idea of the justice perspective. After about a month we added Sr. Margaret to our group. We made a covenant, lasting six months, to gather for one evening a week to pray, dine, and share. We would also meet for one entire day a month for deeper study, prayer, and sharing.

At this time Dan was in charge of Chicago Call to Action, a movement that came out of a national meeting in Detroit in 1976. It was a small group mainly focused on getting Cardinal Cody to be more open and sensitive to the laity and to implement the Vatican II agenda.

Sheila Daley was just getting over burnout from the Church. Like so many other sensitive women, she suffered from the pervasive patriarchy of the Church. Dan and Shelia used our sessions as a launching pad for the transformation of that small, inconsequential local group into one of the most dynamic and progressive groups in the US Church, Call to Action.

Sr. Margaret had just finished several years working with individuals in the Black community who were blind as a result of diabetes. She was an older, mature person who added practical and prayerful suggestions to our development as spokespersons for the justice perspective. After four months her community called her to ministry in Milwaukee.

Here is an example of how we began to articulate the justice perspective. At that time there was a serial killer loose in Atlanta, GA. Twenty-seven young Black males had been murdered. The story saturated the media. At the same time many more than twenty-seven young Black men had been murdered in the Robert Taylor Homes, a notorious Chicago housing project. There was little public knowledge or outcry about this situation which was chronic and repetitive. Meanwhile, 15,000 children around the world were starving to death each week before, during, and after the Atlanta crisis.

We were trying to bring all three horrendous events into a consciousness that would allow people to see in a new way. Things are almost always slanted to protect the rich, powerful, and privileged in society. We needed the skill to surface the deeper, and often, more meaningful aspects of reality so we can respond more appropriately. Our study and prayer was aimed at helping us develop these skills and to teach them to others. This was a concrete example of social analysis.

The 1971 Synod on Justice was an important development in the post-Vatican II understanding of our faith. The Synod developed an iconic statement on justice. It was the clear foundation of the Church's call to a new stance on ministry and the overall practice of our faith, what I call the justice perspective.

"Action on behalf of justice and participation in the transformation of the world fully appear to us as a constitutive dimension of preaching of the Gospel, or, in other words, of the Church's mission for the redemption of the human race and its liberation from every oppressive situation."

This statement is fundamental to all justice and peace ministry practice in the Church. It demands a conversion of one's mentality. Our group sessions were working on this conversion. We got the message but how to make it attractive and acceptable to others was our challenge.

We in the Church carry a legacy that has placed redemption outside of life, outside of the ordinary. This a-historical and other-worldly view of redemption has plagued Christian thought and pastoral practice from the early days of the Church. Until recently, most Christian outlooks have provided no satisfactory opening to the question of Christian responsibility for public life and world history. Our traditional piety and ascetical practices, along with the monopoly of Greek philosophy and Roman theology with its emphasis on the legalistic perspective, confused and obscured the temporal and social dimension of Christ's mission to the world. In a spirituality based on devaluation of sensible reality, there could be little concern for building up the earth and raising standards of living.

Life here was seen as an exile in a valley of tears. What was not eternal was a vanity. Given such a crippling mentality, involvement was difficult for the serious Christian. The tendency was to accept poverty, injustice, oppression, and the political status quo. The result was conservatism and immobilism which prevented the force of the Gospel from transforming the world.

The Synod, following Vatican II, has taught us that redemption is historical. It takes place in life. It is not just a personal and loving relationship with God but a whole plan of human history coming to a conclusion. Everything in this world is called into this plan of redemption. All our social relationships, all our economics, all our politics are called by the saving and mysterious presence of God to the liberation from sin and its consequences and to a celebration of life.

As we grew in this new justice perspective, Shelia, Dan, and I established the Spirituality and Justice Center. From the beginning we wanted to avoid the trap of being an action group unconnected to a deeper spirituality.

We had a definite constituency. They were progressive, white, middleclass Catholics inspired by Vatican II theology and vision. They were seeking a better way to understand and live their faith. In particular, we attracted many who were anxious to deal with sexism in the Church and in society. There was openness to the race issue but the passion of the sixties had dissipated.

We began to have meetings at the center every other Sunday evening. We started with the process of social analysis. This was an analyzing tool that helped people see deeper into their reality.

The first step is experience. People need to name all the factors contributing to their life situation. The more elaborate the details, the better the results.

Secondly, there is the actual social analysis which tries to name the historical and structural elements of the reality. Social analysis searches for what causes the problem. It may be a situation like unequal pay for women doing the same work as men, the continual problem of poor quality education in the inner city, a pattern of segregation in housing or some other social problem. What structures tend to support and continue the unfair circumstances? What issues surface as you ponder the situation? Social analysis searches for what policies cause the problem. What concerns surface? What are the structures behind the experience?

Social analysis will lead to the discovery of structures that are economic, political, cultural, or a mix of these elements. Through these structures the goods of society are facilitated or hindered in their delivery to a specific people. Justice or injustice has its roots in structures that any given segment of society experiences. With the ability to name and grasp the structures, people begin to own their reality, and more importantly, they are on the road to meaningful change in their reality.

The third step in social analysis is theological reflection. In the context of prayer and reading the scripture, people identify what faith has to say about their situation. New themes rise to the surface; avenues of action come to the fore.

This leads to the fourth step, pastoral planning. Goals and objectives are incorporated into a plan of action. Here justice and peace become central to the faith experience and praxis of the particular Christian community.

In a few months, the people coming to the sessions of the Justice and Spirituality Center got a handle on things and they wanted action. This led to the transformation of Call to Action. It was about to become a voice for justice in the Church and society. It was the beginning of a journey for the Daleys. They had a 100 percent commitment to this movement as a way of serving the Church that was both driving them crazy but which they loved dearly.

I accompanied them for the next five years, but I had a different path ahead of me. They retired some thirty years later leaving a legacy to the Church in the United States.

Other Developments

I continued a program of personal study and prayer. I worked with different groups of Carmelites on projects at their schools and parishes. Once a month I mailed out articles on the justice perspective selected from various magazines to all the Carmelites. I developed a weekend retreat which was structured to draw the participants into a more socially conscious experience of their faith. I held these retreats twice a month. They took place at either St. Clara or St. Victor. Soon, different groups of religious invited me to help with their program of justice and peace. Parishes also began to request my growing expertise with their social and justice committees and programs.

Who's the Quarterback?

In the summer of 1979 I attended three week workshop for forty justice and peace leaders of religious orders and congregations. The majority were women religious.

We were assigned groups for discussion after each presentation. Half way through the event I was becoming aggravated with one nun in my group. It seemed she challenged anything I said. Her name was Sister Julia Anne, the same name as my fourth grade teacher who had the triangular ruler.

One morning, I woke up from a dream telling myself that *"she (Sr. Julia Anne) does not realize that I am the quarterback!"*

In a flash, I recognized that was the problem. I was the pushy, male cleric taking over the conversation with minimal regard for the women. Sr. Julia Anne was not accepting the *status quo* with the priest in charge! This experience led me to float up many sexist attitudes and assumptions that were ingrained in my world view. It was the beginning of a personal conversion I had preached to everyone else!

The experience was a perfect example of consciousness raising that I had proclaimed for a couple of years. Sr. Julia Anne gave me a painful initiation by calling me into the light and out of the darkness that so pervades the male-dominated Catholic Church.

Reagan and the Nukes

When President Reagan was elected in 1980, he brought on a crisis in our nuclear policy. He wanted to place missiles with nuclear warheads in Europe. The response in Europe was spontaneous and almost universally opposed. Here in the US, it sparked a small but growing and vocal opposition.

This issue was central for our work in justice and peace and for the Call to Action. Even the US Bishops became engaged and assigned Cardinal Bernadin to prepare a Pastoral Letter on the issue.

I soon became quite informed and vocal on the danger of nuclear arms. I developed a presentation on the topic and gave several talks to those attending our regular meetings.

I then sought to expand the audience. I went to several priest friends and asked to make presentations in their parishes.

At the first five parishes not a single person came in spite of good organization and advertising. In the sixth parish, I had a decent turnout that included an outside, conservative "right to life" group that followed me to all my other talks to make sure I was not handing over the country to the communists.

This process exemplified the changing political climate. The nation was slowly waking to the potential of nuclear war. Reagan's saber rattling began to frighten a large segment of the population.

Besides the increasing number of talks I gathered a small committee of priests to draft an anti-nuclear peace statement. A center piece of the powerful statement was a quote from Pope John XXIII: "…*the arms race should cease; the stockpiles which exist in various countries should be reduced equally and simultaneously... Nuclear weapons should be banned.*"[10]

We also quoted President Eisenhower: "*Every gun that is made, every warship launched, every rocket fired signifies, in the final sense, a theft from those who hunger, and are not fed, who are cold and not clothed.*"[11]

Three hundred and eight priests in the archdiocese signed the document which was published as a full page ad in the Chicago Sunday papers on October 11, 1981. I enjoyed particularly that Leo Mahon and John Malley, two important people in my life, followed each other alphabetically on the list.

Among the many responses to the ad was a call from a group called Mothers for Peace. These women had sponsored activities for many years, including an annual March for Peace, the Saturday before Mother's Day. They wanted me to help organize the 1982 event. I agreed.

Over the next several months I became engrossed in reaching out to parishes and Catholic groups to preach and teach the message of peace. I began to feel the strength of the wind at our back moving from a strong breeze to a gale force. Even the "truth squad" that followed me was getting less rabid.

In all of this I was working with Call to Action which was growing steadily in numbers, organization, and sophistication under the guidance of Dan and Shelia Daley.

As the day of the march approached, I told everybody who would listen that they were in for a surprise. Indeed, they were. The traditional *Mothers' for Peace March* had averaged 500 over the previous ten years. On the day of the March, we had 50,000. I was asked to be the Grand Marshal and reluctantly accepted.

Then the fun began. Everyone wanted to take credit for the phenomenal success. Eventually a committee of representatives from seven groups was established to follow up and organize for the future. From the beginning the meetings were chaotic. Two of the groups professed to be communist. After two months the committee dissolved and the seeds of a larger peace movement were destroyed.

Later on we learned that one of the communist groups that was especially disruptive was a front for the FBI.

Also at this time, there was a civil war raging in El Salvador. There was growing awareness of the horror of this war.

Meanwhile Call to Action put its focus for the next year on the upcoming pastoral letter of the bishops. This long campaign of support concluded with a march of 1,500 on the Sunday afternoon before the gathering of the bishops on May 2, 1983. It is easy for me to remember the day vividly. We had the heaviest rain I ever experienced.

Carmelite Development

One of the great blessings for me was that I was assigned full time as director of justice and peace in our province during the years I was on our provincial council from 1978 to 1984. I started a series of events and projects to educate the men of the province on the issues of justice and peace. In the summers of 1980 and 1981 I conducted week long workshops that eventually involved 80 men of the province. They had an experience of the justice perspective and a call to involvement. One of the men was Ernie Larkin, my intermittent spiritual director and the leading scholar on our prayer tradition. This workshop had a profound effect on him that influenced his teachings in the future. In a few years all our high schools began to show progress in this new area. Besides service projects, justice and peace became part of the regular curriculum.

Around this time Fr. Jack Welch wrote the first of his award winning books, *Spiritual Pilgrims: Carl Jung and Teresa of Avila.*[12] I found it very helpful. It was part of our understanding and articulation of the Carmelite life and charism that was growing throughout the Order. I was one of the many beneficiaries of this movement.

In the general chapter of the entire Order in 1983, Carlos Mesters, a Dutch Carmelite and biblical scholar who worked all his life in Brazil, developed the story of Elijah to help us understand our prophetic tradition. This was very influential in the Order's self-understanding.

Starting in 1980 I began doing summer workshops with the novices. I have continued my work with young Carmelites in initial formation to this day.

Finally during this time I developed the practice of a poustina day. This idea came from Catherine de Hueck. She led a group of lay people in a special life committed to living the Gospel. The day was like a desert day in the city. It was a day removed for any work and ministry to be free for silence and to pray and reflect on one's life. I tried to do one of these days each week. I came closer to getting two a month but in the end, they proved to be a lifesaver.

Arrivals I

One evening in January 1982, a fellow came to the door and asked if he could talk to me. It was strange because he was white and did not look like he wanted a handout.

After a brief introduction, he got down to business, very serious business that was going to influence both of our lives and countless others besides. He wanted to join the Carmelites. Likewise, he wanted to come and live with us at St. Clara right away for several months before he started his formal training in the fall. He wanted to use his time with us at St. Clara to finish his dissertation. He was about to conclude seven years of study to earn a doctorate in anthropology under the guidance of Victor Turner, a world-renowned anthropologist at our neighbor, the University of Chicago. The young man's name was David Blanchard.

Dave had attended the Carmelite minor seminary in Hamilton, Massachusetts, and one year of college with us at Marquette University before he left. Now, he was returning and it was a great day for the Carmelites and for me.

Dave is one of my best friends, the kind you could be away from for six months and smoothly continue the conversation in the middle of the paragraph without missing a beat.

Dave moved in the next day and, very shortly, I had my first experience of what I call "the white tornado." He is an amazingly gifted person with a very broad set of human talents. My first experience was with our monastery. He made an immediate and total transformation: spatial arrangements, messaging and phone system, the library and meeting rooms to share a few. Next, was the worship space. The parish programs came in for the golden touch. At the same time Dave was finishing his dissertation. This was just a warm up for his return a year later.

Dave returned for a year in July 1984, after his novitiate. We learned that the first go-round was indeed just a warm up.

When the year at St. Clara was over, Dave returned to finish his theological studies. As a student, he also became a professor in missiology and Christian anthropology. Eventually, Dave went to El Salvador where for the past twenty-six years he has become a legendary figure in the Church of that nation.

Arrivals II

Connie Driscoll arrived at the Loretto nuns' convent next to Mt. Carmel High School in October 1982. She came to recover from burnout during a project she created for homeless women in Colorado. Probably she collapsed for reasons of her unrestrained personality.

Hollywood would be hard pressed to create a character like Connie. She came from a military career that included a stint in the CIA. She had had a severe stroke in which she lost her left eye and wore a black patch over it. The high powered roman candles of July 4th were like weak sizzlers compared to the ordinary and not infrequent release of Connie's short fuse. Her creativity and energy, at times, seemed limitless, as did her charm when the occasion demanded it.

So after several months of rest, prayer, and a new friend, Sr. Therese O'Sullivan, Connie was ready to tackle a new project in Woodlawn. She opened a storefront shelter down the street from our church and rectory.

Within three months she expanded the storefront to four storefronts and an upstairs. She had encounters of varying degrees of sensitivity with the police, the clients, the parishioners, and the pastor. She recruited support from a large number of progressive nuns, made great connections with the local funders, got the story out in the press, and had time for a scotch or three in the evening. In the meanwhile, her greatest coup was to recruit Sr. Therese from a twenty-seven year career as a first grade teacher. Therese was the best thing that ever happened to Connie and helped her weather many a storm, most self-produced. The new partnership eventually led to the celebration of thirty years of service in the program that became the St. Martin de Porres House of Hope on May 19, 2013.

Early on I went with Connie to a meeting of the funding agencies and various directors of projects. Connie stole the show. Her dominant personality sparkled. I told her that her calling was to work getting the resources and not with the direct service to the women. Within a few weeks she acknowledged that reality. She became a marvelous organizer and executive who produced great resources for the program. Within a few years the archdiocese gave them the old St. Clara School building. This expanded their space thirtyfold.

Sr. Therese worked the floor and came to know the women with deep and loving insight. Over the next few years, the program transitioned from an acceptance of any woman in crisis to victims of domestic violence to throw-away pregnant teenagers and finally, exclusively to women in need of rehabilitation from addiction. That focus has continued to be fine-tuned over the years.

Through her work in development Connie found her real stride working with the conservative group, Acton Institute. She brought substantial funding to the center and some very interesting people came along. Supreme Court Justice Clarence Thomas was among the persons she befriended. Another was Cardinal Lopez Trujillo in Rome. One fascinating story, typical of so many in the extraordinary world Connie created, was about the future Archbishop of Chicago. She asked her Roman Cardinal friend, with whom she conversed often, about who was to be the future Archbishop of Chicago since Cardinal Bernadin was in his final weeks. The Cardinal told her he could not mention the name but said two things. It would be a surprise and the first name and the second name were interchangeable. Six months later, the surprise was real when an unknown bishop, only eleven months as Bishop of Portland, was named to the new role as Archbishop of Chicago, Francis George.

Connie loved the drama but she loved the women in the program even more. She continued to find support for the program. After fifteen years, her health began to decline rapidly, but Connie kept up the effort to the end in 2005.

All this time, her partner, Sr. Therese, was running the day-to-day program and developing her skills in the rehabilitation process and bringing in an increasing number of professionals and outside groups.

Eventually the depth and breadth of the program grew, so that the average client stayed longer, had more programs, and was better equipped to return to the community with a well-founded hope of sobriety. Gradually, the success rate escalated to more than ninety percent.

Today there are hundreds of former residents who have successfully concluded the program and have moved on to a meaningful and productive life. Three have gone on to earn doctorates, a couple hundred have baccalaureate degrees, even more have other credentials ranging from medical assistants to beauticians. All leave the shelter with at least a GED, a high school equivalency credential.

In the meanwhile Sr. Therese has expanded the staff, taken over most of the administration, and works steadily to minimize the daily crises.

When they celebrated their 30th anniversary, the clients recalled with joy and wonder the tender, compassionate, and ever so firm guidance and support of the little lady who transformed their lives. The story of Lazarus is a daily occurrence at the residence. Sr. Therese is the dispenser of both daily miracles and bus tokens in the order they are needed. A day with Sr. Therese is like a journey through chapter 25 of St. Matthew's Gospel with a dry sense of humor. After a thirty-year run, the show is still fresh and exciting with new drama each day. Christmas comes for Sr. Therese many times each year when a client is given money for the first time since beginning the program and returns home sober.

8

LIFE AND DEATH

"I have today set before you life and prosperity, death and doom."
Deuteronomy 30:15

During my years on the provincial council (1978-84) and as pastor of St. Clara-St. Cyril (1984-89), I kept a strong public image as a serious and committed Carmelite. Within my soul and heart, and indeed, my body, there was a ferocious battle going on that led to a lifestyle that was a gross contradiction of that public image. Somewhere within that time frame, I went from a person who had a drinking problem to a full-fledged alcoholic.

To show the contradictions and the confusion this produced in my life, I would like to start out with a reflection on Peter. Peter is portrayed in the Gospels as a true manifestation of our humanity with its strengths and weaknesses, foibles, and nobility.

On the positive side Peter repeatedly comes across as generous, committed and recognized by Jesus as special. When called, Peter did not negotiate. He left the boat and nets behind. He walked with Jesus in simplicity and generosity for almost the entire public life. On several occasions Peter was chosen to be in a small group such as the raising of Jairus' daughter and the Transfiguration. He came up with the right answer when Jesus asked the big question. "Who do you say that I am?"

On the negative side, Peter was never far from putting his foot in his mouth. He started to walk on the water only to lose faith and start to sink. He told Jesus he did not have to suffer and die. He rejected the call to walk to Jerusalem, which is the heart of Jesus' message, and pleaded that they should settle down on Mt. Tabor. At the washing of the feet Peter first denies Jesus' plea only to turn around and ask him to wash the entire body.

Then there is the classic event. Only a few hours after Jesus foretold Peter's rejection, Peter flees the garden where he slept while Jesus prayed in agony. Then he wilts in fear from the poor maid, "I do not know the man." Three times, no less!

Peter, who had been at the side of Jesus for most of his public life, shared meals with him and walked countless miles in dialogue and searching conversation with the Savior of the world. He had witnessed his many healings, his walking on the water, the feeding of the multitudes and so much more. He was at the tomb when Lazarus came out. He was present for the first Eucharist with Jesus just hours earlier, and then he says, "I do not know the man." Three times no less!

After the resurrection Jesus appears to Peter and the others. Jesus does not say what most of us would say, "You thick headed, ignorant man. I taught you and shared with you and accepted you. I explained to you three times that I had to go Jerusalem to suffer and die so I could rise. You respond after all of this, 'I do not know the man.' What a waste of time!"

No, none of this was on Jesus' agenda. He said simply, "Peace be with you." This is followed in John by the story of the threepeat where he asks Peter: do you love me? On the third question Peter gets upset! This is just forty-eight hours from his famous fold, "I do not know the man." Now Peter is upset. How blind can he be?

Peter's blindness is only overcome by the mercy and compassion of Jesus. Peter's story is my story at all times but most especially between 1978 and 1989. True self-knowledge is a precious gift that comes very slowly.

BEGINNING

During parts of my journey, I have kept a journal. Almost all of its entries consist of reflections on retreats and special days of prayer, the poustina days. I started the poustina day in the beginning of 1980 as my commitment to prayer as part of the prayer and reflection center at St. Clara. These special days proved to be a lifesaver for me in many ways.

I did not have any journal notes from October 1978, until I began again in July 1982. In my 1978 notes I had two small items about my drinking.

For several entries in my journal, beginning in July 1982, I listed a deep concern about my lifestyle and the use of money and my lack of "fire in the belly" for the poor. Over all there was a deep sense of dissatisfaction with my way of living.

Then on October 17, 1982, I wrote the following:

"This has been a good day with many insights. I guess the most important one is that I am really much more broken and weak than I realize. It seems that my illusions about myself just cannot stand the light of day but I hide behind the practices (spiritual activities) especially morning prayer and the poustina day. But I am not involved in many things so I won't be "too busy" or "too stretched out" and then I use the time I save to drink and relax! The depth of my self-deception, about the fact that I'm just not the great guy and great radical people think I am, slowly came into a better focus. I have a drinking problem. I have a choice between my 'prayer' and my life symbolized by my overweight, 203 [pounds], and my nose cosmetics! I've got to be more accepting of my reality and recognize my weakness and phoniness and honest to God laziness! I need to change but the first thing I need to do is accept my situation and turn to Jesus. I'm not going to earn his love. All I need to do is accept myself as I am and break out of my illusions – but they are so enormously engulfing! – and let Jesus be my savior. The issue on the surface is lifestyle but down deep it is my need to recognize and accept my weakness and self-deception and turn to Jesus in my brokenness. Help me Lord!"

Between October 17th and November 1st there were two entries that generally were about my feeling out of sorts, not working, and not being energized. There was a growing sense of confusion between my self-image and the reality of my life. Then on November 1st, I had this to say:

"There is a very clear and powerful message today. I have to stop drinking! Of all the things in my life, drinking is the single biggest obstacle to my seeking the Kingdom. It is the biggest attraction into illusions and away from reality. It is the greatest desolation. Besides, it is becoming clearer by the hour that I can't drink. This is a new awareness. Once I have a drink, I stay drinking, no matter how lightly, for the rest of the evening. More and more, I think about drinking when I think about going to some event. It is clearly a sign of real brokenness within me and a draw to greater and greater selfishness. I simply have to quit drinking if I'm going to seek the Kingdom. The choice has never been so clear. Please help me Lord.

Drinking is right at the heart of the lifestyle program I've been struggling with and the obstacle to being in solidarity with the poor. Right now I feel very much as a beginner but I feel good that the choice is so clear. Please help me not to deceive myself, Lord. I have to change and only God's grace can deliver me from my brokenness and addiction.

This has been coming on for several weeks, if not months now, but NOW is the acceptable time. Today is the day of salvation, let us be glad and rejoice in it. No drink is going to bring me closer to the Kingdom or more in solidarity with the poor or make me think clearer. Lord that I may see and seeing may choose life!"

This is where Peter moves in. It would have been a great story if Peter went with Jesus to Jerusalem with no hesitation and no doubt. Can you not imagine a Hollywood Peter saying at the foot of the cross, "Let me get another cross so they can crucify me also." Well, Peter did die on the cross but only after a journey of self-knowledge and growth in trust and love. In the meanwhile we have the beautiful story of his human frailty to help us on the way. I sure was going to need all the help I could get to move from the clarity of my insight about the disaster of my drinking to the reality of stopping.

On the one side was the clarity of the mind's insights. On the other side was the power of my feelings and the overwhelming addiction of the body with its blinding and overpowering attraction. Herein lays the source of the contradictions in the life of the alcoholic. I did not know it at the time, but through the miracle of God's grace, I was just beginning the path to freedom.

At the end of December 1982, I went on a three day retreat with Fr. Ernie Larkin, the spiritual director who helped at many critical points in my life. I told him I had a drinking problem and I opened myself up to him in a very deep way, telling him of the violation of my vow of chastity at times when I was drinking heavily. He told me I need to work to get more affect in my prayer and he pointed out that one of my problems was that I wanted to be the perfect Carmelite and should accept my weakness more openly. He told me to pray and ponder the truth of God's love for me.

One point I was struggling with was to get more energy to address the activities that I was neglecting or performing poorly. I became aware that I would lose my moral compass when I drank.

I did not realize that drinking was having a profound impact on my personality. At times, I felt I was carrying a big gorilla on my back. This awareness would grow over the coming months and years. Of course, I had a one liner in my notes on this entry, "I started to drink again." This captured the paradox that was my life at the time.

Once again, I tried to face up to the fact that I cannot drink. On March 17, 1983, I wrote,

"What has been surfacing the last week or so is what the case was last November 1982. I can't drink and be faithful to pursuing the Lord. I have to let go. Right now the most anti-Kingdom thing in my life is drinking and the self-absorption in produces in me. I need to change. I need to move on. I need to sell. I've been here before and I always fall back. I have to let go and trust the Lord. It cannot be a moralistic decision but an opening up to the call, to the Lord's love, to entering into the Mystery. It is not often that the choice and the issue are so clear but I have great and almost insurmountable skills at self-deception. If I do, I'll just have to admit my weakness and start over again because in our weakness we find our strength. In the meanwhile, I have to do everything I can to seek the Kingdom, to let go, and concretely, right now, that means to quit drinking and to accept the void that produces in my life. Please be with me Lord so I may become free to really open my life to the needs of my sisters and brothers!"

MIDDLE

I reported the same theme on April 15th and several other entries in the journal leading up to February 25, 1984. On February 22nd, Jack Egan, though indirectly, came into my life at another serious juncture. Early in his career he had started the Cana Conference, a program to help couples prepare for marriage. On that day, I received a newsletter from Cana that was on alcoholism. It included a test. I took the test. I failed!

On February 25th I wrote,

> "That afternoon walking by the lake, I was able to admit that I am an alcoholic. Then, Thursday, I searched out this truth. I've waited a few days to write this down because so many times in the past I would admit to drinking problems on a poustina day and then proceed to go on drinking at the next opportunity.

One of the mos: helpful insights was the number of times I admitted to myself the presence of a drinking problem and specifically on Nov. 1, 1982, and April 15, 1983. I clearly stated in writing in this book that I was not able to drink.

There are several points I want to make:

One major item that struck me in the Cana document is that alcoholism is a disease that is Progressive, Insidious, and Changes The Way One Thinks.

Progressive: there is absolutely no doubt that I am not able to drink the way I could. Each time now I want to drink to conclusion which is either to go out or until I go to bed. Once I have a drink, even though I still have control when I have a drink, I drink the rest of that day. There is no more work, study, or prayer.

A second part of progressive is the dependency on alcohol for relaxation and recreation. My control of drinking is 80-90% before the first drink. On the other hand, I never drink before work of any sort. But the amount of time wasted when I drink does affect the quality of work by cutting into preparation time and my physical condition such as being tired.

INSIDIOUS: The self-deception is so massive and so contrary to what I say I want to do with my life that only grace can let me see it. There is no doubt that the single biggest obstacle for me in seeking to walk with Jesus is alcohol and how it permeates my life and lifestyle and yet I continue to work and pray in almost total blindness to this reality in many of the days of my life. The contradiction is blatant but almost hidden from me. Over the last 16 months I must have "stopped" drinking 7 or 8 times only to turn around and have the first drink, which I know in my heart, is going to lead to several weeks of escalation until the contradiction leads me to either stop praying and reflecting or face the issue. BUT IT IS INSIDIOUS!

IT CHANGES THE WAY YOU THINK!: All my values and mindset are seriously but subtlety lost and distorted after one or two drinks and this grows more so in a way that I am almost another person. No doubt, I began operating out of some unconscious part of my personality in a very unhealthy way. This is easily excused and passed off without much guilt the next day even though it holds the potential of great damage to me and so many I love and respect. The latest episode probably led me to stop drinking the last three months. I stopped drinking on Dec. 1 and started Dec. 11 and this culminating in me going out after 8 PM and having the house robbed by the time I returned three hours later. This led me to stop drinking for a month, and then I drank heavily for a couple of weeks. This was probably why I was open to read the Cana document.

What is new at this time is that I am willing not only to admit that I cannot drink but that I am an alcoholic with a disease that is progressive, insidious, and changes the way I think when drinking.

I have been able to turn to Jesus and offer myself as I am and beg for help. I know I can't drink, and, in fact, in spite of the lapses there has been growing progress in identifying the problem. Ernie told me to trust in the Lord and not move to a quick moralistic solution. His advice has been a help in letting me see my utter weakness and helplessness. It has been a hindrance in not stopping my drinking and, in fact is being used as an excuse for my drinking. Another real sign of progress is coming to realize I am wrong in drinking and not turning to Jesus for forgiveness and help.

The question is, what to do? I do know there is enormous spiritual pride and I do not want to go public at this time but the reality is that I'll probably fall again till I realize I can't do it by myself. It would be great if I could simply turn to the Lord in trust and completely surrender but my history shows this to be unlikely though I will try.

What I propose to do is try it out for a few weeks and see what happens.

I did not know it at the time, but looking from a distance, the event of the Cana document and reflection was the beginning of the end. I was going to ride the roller coaster of starting and stopping drinking for the next four and a half years. However, there was a slow, steady progress. There were longer periods of abstinence. During these periods, some crucial healing was taking place.

I finally shared my condition of being an alcoholic with my community two months later in May and I continued to stay in touch with Ernie Larkin.

END

I was blessed with community and friendship at this time. It was the beginning of my time as pastor. In August 1984, John Rivera and Dave Blanchard joined Marco Pardo and Andy Skotnicki to form the best community I have had in my life as a Carmelite. There was much sharing and prayer and a lot of intellectual curiosity which began to draw me out of my self-absorption. George O'Keefe kept his eye on me and even intervened, only to be confronted by my denial. Nevertheless, George hung in with me. At the same time my sister, Sister Therese, always offered a gentle and encouraging word and even a gentle correction when needed.

With the gift of hindsight I wonder why I did not go to AA. It was probably spiritual pride. I guess the Lord took some of the pride and ran it through the ringer in the next few years because the struggle and pain continued.

Another thought was that the prayer and reflection of the poustina days I was into the twelve steps before I knew I was an alcoholic. This was, in the end, both a lifesaver and an invitation to grow more deeply in trust in God because I slowly learned that *"Let go, and let God"* is the only way.

Two meaningful insights have helped me face my reality. One is from Gerald May's *Addiction and Grace*.[13] He pointed out that the brain is deeply affected by the alcohol. It develops an urgent physical need as the consumption of alcohol increases. Therefore, the brain is working 24 hours a day to satisfy this longing. It develops a wide range of mind tricks to convince the person to drink in spite of all the goodwill to the contrary. Therefore, it is an uphill battle to close the deal on the termination of the drinking, no matter how clear and intense the good intentions are.

The second item was from an article that I discovered in the Spring, 1985, Notre Dame Alumni magazine. After I read this article, I realized that this was God's answer to my three Hail Marys in 1945 when I asked what kind of God could let Notre Dame be beaten 59-0 by Army. Now I knew what kind of God, a God who was walking me through the valley of darkness into the light.

The thing I feared most about my disease was being out of control. I had the potential to harm many people. I also felt a continual lethargy and lack of passion about things I once had held dearly. The gorilla was weighing me down. The Notre Dame article pointed out that recovery was more than just abstinence from alcohol. The recovering person has regained the ability to exercise various human potentials. Fr. Bill Stenzel goes on to say:

"It has to do with the wholeness of the person…recovery has to include physical health, emotional health and spiritual health…Recovery has everything to do with helping the person to become who he or she has the potential to be."

Over the next four and half years I struggled with a pattern of stop and go feeding of the beast. My only conclusion is that God knew I needed to get a glimpse that I am not in control. I finally had my last drink, *to date*, on August 20, 1989. It was the night before I reported to my assignment to work with the formation program of the Carmelite theology house at Whitefriars Hall. It was interesting in that it was a single drink and no more to follow up. That pattern of reducing most drinking periods had been increasing for about three years. There were longer periods without drinking and then, when I did drink, it was most often at home and with less consumption. While abstinence grew, so did the process of healing.

An example of that was an insight I journaled on May 8, 1986. Part of my sickness was projection and being judgmental about those I differed with in any way. Fr. Nelson, the pastor I lived with from 1978 to 1984, was the victim of my rash judgments but there were many others I judged harshly. Only slowly was I able to see that there are many sides to the story beyond my view. This particular day this insight came into full view. I had a difficult encounter with the principal of the grammar school who was in his final three weeks because we had deep disagreement on most issues. I wrote this:

> "Today there were a series of conflicts with Tom. My motor started running and I was becoming angrier and obsessed with the chaos that comes from him. Then I had an insight and a grace. Indeed, the situation was evil but so are all kinds of other situations such as the nuclear incident in Russia, the cases of the women in the shelter, Reagan's cuts against the poor, and so on. It is my selfishness that distorts the situation with Tom. It is a sinful situation and it will be a sinful situation when Tom is gone. What makes it so bad is my exaggerated self-importance and self-righteousness. Help me Lord to see this more clearly and to respond with love and not vengeance. My, I have a long way to go!

> I had a deep desire to come home and drink after the meeting. It was as if all I was thinking and praying and writing for the last week and half were non-existent. No wonder they say one day at a time. This disease is incredibly insidious. Help me Lord Jesus!

I had a very intense experience during a retreat at the Trappist Monastery in New Mellary, Iowa in July 1988. To this point I was in a slow but steady healing process. These eight days were special and intensified a growth pattern that is still in effect today, twenty-five years later.

> "I feel many things;

> I am young and just beginning the journey. I have enthusiasm and desire

and determination to seek the Lord and his Kingdom;

I need to work at integrating John of the Cross and Lonergan's program of the transcendental precepts;

I need to develop new skills and new intellectual curiosity;

A pattern of many central ideas (from reading all my previous journals) that surface over and over again is captured in John and Lonergan;

I need to recognize daily that I am an alcoholic. About the only time I do is when I am writing. Thank God for at least that. I need to share it openly with my community and be out front about my sneaking drinks. It has to stop. All else is a joke if I don't;

The pattern I had discerned is one of slow and gradual growth with a particularly dangerous period between 1983-85 when I was an incredible contradiction between the progressing alcoholism and the self-perceived "spiritual maturity." It is clear that my strength is my weakness. Thank you, Lord Jesus!

Another passage that revealed that healing is taking place:

"First of all some themes that have appeared over and over again in my notes, such as "bachelor lifestyle," "work and change," and "passion for a project" all came into a clearer focus.

"Bachelor lifestyle" has tremendously deep roots within me. I see it more and more as a deeply rooted selfishness and a drying up, a fear of life. It is characterized by deep patterns of comfort and control that so permeate my life. The drinking pattern was so pervasive and dominant that when it began to cool down other patterns surfaced. Examples are my dependence on TV sports, eating alone, quality of friendships, and many more.

A dimension of this is having my activities and responsibilities in the parish and community be things that have to get "done" – so I can go back to loafing and relaxing. Underlying this attitude is a lack of love and fear of personal involvement that keeps me from giving people real quality time and presence. The dominating reality is my "schedule" and my "time." This was pointed out so clearly when I did give of myself in the parish pilgrimage to Niagara.

It is obvious that I need to change. It seems that a combination of John's Program and Lonergan's transcendental precepts hold a key to what direction to go.

The two other themes that showed up in the notes "work and change" and "a sense of passion" seem to trigger some very deep challenges to me at this time.

"Work and change" seems to be a call to break out of the very comfortable and basically lazy cocoon I have developed for myself. So much of my activity is just getting by, "getting it done," marking off the "things that need to get done." I am more a victim than a liver of life. I need to be more present to my world and quit looking for some great solution around the corner like leaving St. Clara for whatever. I need to plunge into the action and accept the limits and the tensions and the brokenness of the people. This is where God had called me, and when She wants me elsewhere I'll know about it. In the meanwhile, I need to dig in.

A "sense of passion" showed up over and over again in the notes. It was as if I had some romanticized moment in the past when I had it all together and was looking for it to appear again.

What I need is a sense of passion for life now and quit thinking and feeling like an old man. I have cut down my options in interests almost in all directions so I don't do anything new and different. I need to change and open up. A good example is learning how to sing or learning how to use the computer or a thousand other things that I'm so predictable in that they would immediately say, "Tracy wouldn't be interested in that." (Basically, because it would interfere with watching the Sox!)

I am reading the following passage twenty-five years after I first wrote it. I have never lived a day in my life according to the standards I set for myself in the words of this entry. The message is truly beautiful and very much a call into the future for me. While I have not achieved the awesome ideal that it sets forth, there are more and more days that I want to continue the struggle to grasp it. The grace is in the struggle not in the accomplishment.

July 1st: "this is a quote from Lonergan and Spirituality[11]:"Once we let transcendent love find human persons to love, we see a purpose in life beyond being practical and efficient, or being a contributor to a process of communication of information and goods. The larger purpose is simply to love. Our principle of selection changes – selection of what to say in a group, of how to spend a Friday evening, and so on. It is now a method controlled by love and purpose, where intelligence is instrumental. We let go of selecting according to the habit of mere intelligence – what will work most efficiently – without posing the further question of purpose and value. We no longer oscillate between meeting a chain of responsibilities, necessities and obligations, and, on the other hand, loafing, relaxing, storing up for new rounds of duties."

Where to begin? This is so on target!

School Board and Liturgy meetings! – I leave as soon as the business is over; let them turnout the lights! This is a real expression of the reality of getting it done, getting it over with. It is loveless and totally devoid of quality presence to the people. The critical point is that that is characteristic of a great amount of my effort. I can say that my presence at liturgy on Sunday has been changing and growing in this positive direction.

I guess the key point is I need to open my life to simply loving the people and reduce the programs and agenda. This works for all – parish, staff, family, Carmelites, school parents, Woodlawn folks, CDS, etc., etc. I need to change. O Lord, do I need to change. Please help me.

The roots of the bachelor lifestyle are so deep I'll never come close by myself.

I need to change to a contemplative lifestyle that will be open to love and to life, which will work and will play and wonder and waste time with people while starting new things like singing and computers and maybe even chess.

But to do this, I will need to practice John's program and let go of a lot of things! To list a few – sports section, going to the movies alone and a lot less often, visiting family more often, not eating alone, fasting regularly, going over to Carmel (the neighboring Carmelite high school) more often and more suggestions will arise.

It is incredible how deep are the patterns of selfishness and controlled comfort in the bachelor lifestyle I have developed.

It seems the key is love. I have been so busy performing many duties and fighting the big battles: building up the parish, saving the school, and being the ideal Carmelite that I haven't had time for love.

Well, now is a good time to begin. Help me Lord Jesus. One step at a time is the way to go and know I need prayer and sacrifice and discipline but most of all in walking the way of love with Jesus."

Well, chess is still on the waiting list but I have made some progress in a lot of the others.

On my last day of this very special time of my life at the Trappist retreat house, I wrote the following conclusion.

"I'm in my final evening of what has been a very exceptional week. Among the many thoughts on my mind today is the fact that much of what I have suggested to fit a new pattern of behavior has been creeping into my life already. What is different is how clearly I see the need for wide-ranging change and the connectedness of so many activities that I have blocked out in maintaining a very selfish and very rigid and clearly defined (re limits e.g. never during a Bears game!) lifestyle. What I have on my hand now is an incredible infusion of grace and clarity and a call to real change of lifestyle – a lifestyle rooted in a hunger for God and based on self-giving and mortification. It has been amazing to see how my denial of listening to the White Sox has been identical pattern of game-playing similar to when I'm fighting to have a drink.

I have thought about how easy it is to write the stuff down here in the book as I have done in the past and then go home and get swamped by the intensity of the old patterns. But I have noticed that the suggestions that make this book sooner or later have been put into practice. Secondly, I believe the key is a strong commitment to John's program. I really see the need for change. I really want to change. I want to be faithful to prayer, to the community, and to the journal that will help me name and understand the reality that I will be living.

If I go back over the list of particulars, it is large and easily expandable. It comes down to Lonergan's question of authenticity and being faithful to the transcendental precepts in seeking God, in being open to the Mystery in All places and All times and with All people. The obstacles are that my life and my heart are filled with so much garbage and so narrow self-interest that I can't do it – Enter John's Program! Help me Lord, I want to seek you with all my heart, I want to learn how to love so to break loose and love life. Another obstacle is my lazy habits, e.g., getting by with so many things such as teaching a class or a Scripture discussion rather than really making the full effort at every level to really work at it and to be present to the people and to take it seriously as an encounter with the Lord!

Over the last several years, I have felt a burden being lifted from me in terms of work. For whatever reason, I used to really suffer from a split soul: the recruiting for the workshops and work with CTA were examples. Likewise, I had a fear of controversy and conflict, especially with people I work with. These have been gradually going away. Now I feel that I am being called into a new dimension of freedom – a freedom of all kinds of limits and restraints and schedules and sacred times that need to be shattered so I may seek the Lord day and night. My narrow little work world has been called in by the Lord for a total rehab! Help me to be open and committed to the new world Lord. Give me the generosity to be faithful to my Carmelite calling, to be faithful to the Gospel, to be faithful to my mediating on the Law of the Lord night and day – what could be more faithful than being open to the Mystery in all places and times and especially persons. I need to change, and I can with your grace Lord Jesus."

Reflection

On retreat in July 2003, I had one of my clearest experiences of seeing God's action in my life as expressed in the theme of this book, *been there all along.*

The following was in my journal on July 23rd:

"Another theme that sparkled in the re-reading (of my journals) is Exodus 19:4 'Tell the Israelites: you have seen for yourselves how I treated the

Egyptians and how I bore you up on eagle wings and brought you here to myself.'

The healing and the delivery from the slavery of alcoholism is just a story of incredible beauty and grace. I have been thinking of what I would be today if I had not been carried on eagle wings away from the death of alcoholism. It is hard to imagine any greater grace in my life. Indeed, it is a saving God that has born me on eagle wings."

The story of Peter's journey of self-knowledge is very comforting. It is a long journey from hearing the words of Jesus to the time they blossom in one's life. It is a long, hard struggle to embrace the consequences of the Gospel message. I can see that clearly in experiencing the chasm between my insights and good intentions of journal days and the much compromised flow of my daily and very ordinary life. Truly, one will find God in the continuing struggle of our ambiguity and that of others. The Church is for sinners seeking to move away from their self-absorption. Like Peter we all have an immense journey ahead of us. We need to have patience with ourselves and others. We always need to be willing to start over again. The only loss is to quit the struggle because God is in the struggle.

Fr. Tracy's seventh grade class at St. Laurence Catholic School on the southside of Chicago. Tracy is third in the row by the blackboard. (1949)

"This is the only football picture I have." (1953).

(Above) Tracy in his first year of college, wearing the tunic and belt of the Carmelite habit, at the Carmelite seminary in Niagara Falls, Ontario. (December 1954)

(Left) Four O'Sullivan Brothers, 1942: (standing) Tim; (seated l-r): Connie, Joe (Fr. Tracy), and John.

(Right) Fr. Tracy and Sr. Therese meet at the Carmelite dining room at Mount Carmel College in Niagara Falls, Ont. Sr. Therese is a member of the Sisters of Loretto (IBVM) who had a large house next to Mount Carmel.

Eight O'Sullivans: (front row) Ellen Larmon and Mary Heenan; (second row) Peggy Majka, Sr. Therese; (back row): Fr. Tracy, Tim, John, and Connie.

Fr. Tracy watching from the door of St. Clara-St. Cyril parish priory in the Woodlawn neighborhood of Chicago.

Fr. Tracy "in the midst of the people" for a picture at the conclusion of the farewell Mass at St. Clara's-St. Cyril's parish in Chicago's Woodlawn area. (July 1989).

Fr. Tracy with some friends at the St. Clara-St. Cyril parish festival. (July 1990)

Fr. Tracy addressing a gathering of Carmelites during a provincial chapter, the Order's elective and legislative meeting held every three years.

Fr. Tracy in the kitchen area of the home of a parishioner. (2012)

St. Raphael Mariachi-- Jaime Morales, Director and Founder, standing on the far right. Fr. Tracy and Fr. Tom Alkire, the associate pastor, are standing in the back. (2006)

Next Page:

Mr. Peter Scoot and St. Raphael students at Fr. Tracys 75th birthday celebration in October 2010.

(right): Fr. Tracy and a young friend in the prayer garden at St. Raphael's Parish in Los Angeles.

(below): Fr. Tracy celebrating Easter at St. Raphael's Parish in Los Angeles. (2013)

(bottom right) Ms. Ena Duran and Ms. Esther Manriquez during the transiton of two secretaries. (1998)

9

Back As Pastor

When I finished my time on the provincial council, in June 1984, I convinced a reluctant provincial that it would be good for me to return to St. Clara-St. Cyril parish as pastor. He felt it would be good for me to leave Woodlawn after all these years. We were both right but just a little different on the timeline.

When I was installed as pastor in June 1984, Woodlawn was dramatically different from the area I arrived at as a young priest twenty years earlier. "Depopulated" was a major understatement that would describe the reality. The area was in a transition that would take decades. It was slowly but steadily moving from an overcrowded ghetto to a gentrified "Hyde Park South," an extension of the neighborhood to the north that is home to the University of Chicago and the Obama family residence.

The population in 1984 was about one third of what it was at its height of 90,000 in the mid-sixties. A symbol of the new reality was the removal of the "El" tracks on 63rd Street. We were soon in talks about amalgamating our parish with Holy Cross, the parish six blocks to the west.

I had a vision of the parish as a new kind of parish. As always, there was a good sized gap between my vision and the nuts and bolts of a realistic program. I envisioned the parish as a witness against the isolation and segregation of the city. I wanted it to be a place where the worship would include all God's children, Black and White, rich and poor. Inclusiveness was a major priority.

Many rumors preceded my installation. Some were on target and others were petty and destructive. We scheduled a parish meeting the first week in which I laid out my vision. I and the new staff listened to people. They had plenty to say. It was a very dynamic session once we got by the initial apprehension. The parishioners were not terribly excited about my two initiatives to have the Visitors' Sunday and to open up to the women in the rehab center. At the same time they expressed a desire for a more authentically African American liturgy. Jocelyn King, the director of religious education, was a strong and consistent voice on this theme. The parishioners also wanted more, and deeper, faith formation. After more general sessions and work with the pastoral council, we identified some clear parish priorities. Among these were more social activities.

At the same time I was able to gain some support for my dream of a more open and inclusive parish. So I started out with two major initiatives. The first was an open invitation to the metropolitan area to come and join us for Mass with a vibrant African American liturgy and Gospel music on the third Sunday of the month in particular, but any time that was convenient. We called this Visitors' Sunday. The second was a new and enthusiastic reaching out to the women and children in the St. Martin de Porres House of Hope, the rehab center. The neighborhood would give us further opportunities and challenges to flesh out our commitment to being more inclusive. Residents of halfway houses began to attend. Finally, we had a beautiful experience of accepting and supporting a group of gay men in their participation in the parish at all levels.

While the new vision included openness to the wider community and the poorer community, the much more dominant component of the vision, and what the people wanted, was deeper evangelization and formation of the members of the parish which consisted of a few hundred families. The members were predominantly lower middleclass, hardworking, and extremely generous in their support for the parish. Likewise, they were quite open to the programs directed to enrich their faith. They were particularly concerned that the liturgy express the gifts of the African American culture in a Catholic context.

All of this helped me to bring Leo Mahon's vision of proclaiming the Word and Sacrament into an African American Catholic framework.

Therefore, the first item to be addressed was the liturgy. There were four masses on the weekend schedule. None of them had as many as a 120 in attendance on a regular basis. At the initial meeting with the entire parish, we agreed to try for two months to have just one Mass to have better participation, better music, better preparation and overall, livelier liturgy. There was no need for a follow-up meeting because of the enthusiastic embrace of the new liturgy.

While the parish was small by most standards, there was an exceptional level of participation at liturgy, parish ministries, faith formation activities and the busy social calendar of the parish. The result was an extraordinary sense of community and belonging. This all worked to create special feeling that made the Sunday Eucharist clearly the central and uniting event of the parish.

The Carmelite Community

As I began my five years as pastor, I had a marvelous Carmelite community for support. In fact, it proved to be the best community I have ever experienced in all my years as a Carmelite. The prior was Andy Skotnicki. He was a full time chaplain at the Cook County Jail and a very intelligent, gifted, and driven man who at the suggestion of Dave Blanchard was soon to go on to earn a doctorate in social ethics. Marco Pardo was a layman and a friend of Andy. Marco had moved in to live with us the year before. He stayed with the Carmelites in a temporary commitment for ten years both in the parish and later as Hispanic vocation director. He was modeling what I had often thought we should do more of, an open-ended commitment to the religious life. Because he lived in community with us, he shared our life much more fully than a Jesuit volunteer or participants in other programs like that that are abundant these days. Then, there were two Carmelite interns, John Rivera who was teaching full time at Mt. Carmel High School and Dave Blanchard who was working in the parish. Dave was with us for only one year and John for two years before they returned to their theological studies. Finally, Fr. Martin Curtis was an associate pastor but deeply constrained by poor health.

On Tuesday morning each week, we shared the scripture readings of the coming Sunday. On Thursday afternoon, we shared some relevant book or article like Merton's *Contemplative Prayer* or Galilea's *The Future of Our Past*. These sessions led to a deep sharing of our lives and a great mutual support system.

I was strong on the vision. Marco and Dave were strong on the practical and programmatic expression. With the flow of these three strong personalities, the circus was definitely in town. I soon learned that anytime Dave started to give an extended dissertation on some seemingly remote point, it meant two things: a profound change was on the way and I better get the checkbook ready for a big hit!

One of the first of these anthropological experiences was about the difference between sign and symbol. The worship space was cluttered with little banners from all the groups in the parish. Dave said they had to go. In came the symbol.

To my utter amazement, I got an $8,000 bill for cloth. Then, I saw the cloth, hanging majestically in five columns above the sanctuary. The strips were 48 inches wide and 40 yards in length. We had an extremely high ceiling. The cloths completely transformed the space. They were an almost hidden but intense invitation into a sense of the sacred in the plain colors of the liturgical season.

On another occasion Dave developed an entire Advent program around an obscure part of the liturgy, the *O Antiphons*, which proved to be a great and enlightening invitation into the biblical message of the Advent Season.

Marco was a trained and experienced counselor. He was much more hands on in his approach, developing parenting programs and RCIA activities that supported a steady flow of new members into the parish community. His specialty was music, both sacred and profane. He had a very fine Gospel choir but his true love was a group that included most of his choir members called "The Oldies But Goodies" which specialized in the rock and roll tunes of the sixties. Like anywhere, good music leads to a sense of community. Marco had a very special gift of bringing the music into a Gospel call to break down the barriers.

These examples from Dave and Marco were just symbols of what they brought to the parish.

The main activity was the evangelization and formation of the people. At all levels, we wanted people to grow in their faith. In liturgy, many worked for the certificates the archdiocese gave for the various liturgical ministries. We had programs for all the catechists. We did a special, prolonged workshop on the Bishops' pastoral letter on the economy. We had many workshops on prayer and Carmelite spirituality and, of course, on the Bible. The emphasis was to bring the Word of God into all expressions of our personal and parish activity. Most of all, it was the inclusiveness of the expanded vision as we celebrated the Eucharist. Visitors' Sunday and the women from the shelter and the guests from our neighborhood community made the Body of Christ more real and tangible for all of us.

Sharing Program

We inherited a mature and well developed Sharing Program with St. Anne parish in Barrington, Illinois, 65 miles away. This was the source of many activities and support for the parish and especially the school. One, in particular, was an employment program.

One of the parishioners of St. Anne had a factory that re-cycled large batteries. This involved hard work. He had a tough time getting sufficient workers. He proposed that we get some of our unemployed men to fill this void. He offered to help with transportation and to pay them well.

He gave the parish a fifteen passenger van and set one requirement for the workers. They had to pass a drug test. We soon had a clear picture of the depth of poverty in our community.

The son of one of our active parishioners asked me to help him by getting him a pass for the drug test. I did not. It was no problem getting fifteen workers to start. Soon, there was a filtering pattern in place. Roughly one third of the workers before long went on to higher level of work in the factory and got their own transportation. One third stayed at the entry level of work with varying degrees of difficulty. One third of the candidates could not cut it at all and were quickly released or dropped out. This pattern held steady for three years until there was no need for more employees.

Food Pantry

Another program the sharing parish helped with was with our food pantry. Through St. Anne parishioners we contacted food companies and food distributors that were great resources for our food program.

Our food pantry was well organized and well stocked. We distributed between twelve and fourteen tons of food each month. Also, in collaboration with other community churches, we had a large hot meal for several hundred people once a week.

The recipients of the food had a regular schedule for their pick-up every two weeks. They were grateful for the help. On two occasions they returned the favor when given the opportunity.

One Sunday at 1 AM, I heard a strange noise outside my window. I looked out and saw someone driving my car away. That evening, Marco saw the car in traffic but it was going in the opposite direction and he could not maneuver a turn to catch up with it.

On Monday we asked all the clients of the food pantry to help us find Fr. Tracy's car. By 11 AM we had a location.

I called the police. An African American woman officer came quickly and I went with her a few blocks away. Parked in the hidden service entrance of an old building was my car. I had not brought my keys. The officer said I could save her a lot of paper work if I let her hotwire my car. I did so gladly. It was one of the more enjoyable moments of my tenure at the parish to "steal" my car back. My only regret was not being able to see the look on the thief's face when he arrived to see the car gone.

Another time I was giving a week long workshop to our novices on justice and peace and the Carmelite life. On the last night a man broke into the rectory and eventually came to the only bedroom on the first floor. A novice was sleeping there. He was awakened and threatened and terrified into four hours of silence while the burglar went about his search.

The novice finally woke me at 6 AM. We examined the premises and only some frozen meat and two old chalices from the chapel were missing. We called the police. The officers were both Catholic and took it personally that the chalices were part of the theft.

Once again, we went to the food pantry for help. There were usually between thirty-five and fifty clients each day. This was quite adequate to get the word out to the community, much better than the newspaper or cable TV!

In the early afternoon, we had a response. A large and unusual BBQ was sighted on 66th St. Once again we called the police. The same officers were still on duty. They returned in an hour with some of the meat and, much to the joy of the young policemen, the two chalices.

Visitors' Sunday

This program of an open invitation to the wider community to join us for Mass on the third Sunday built up slowly. We eventually had over two hundred visitors each month.

We tried to build up a deeper connection through programs and workshops. One that was quite successful was the presentation on the Bishops' pastoral letter on the economy. In the long run, however, there was no structure to sustain a relationship with the visitors. We had the structures with the many programs and activities of the sharing program such as the parish picnics, school visits, confirmation service programs and retreats and many more. In fact, we even began a new sharing program with a city parish, St. Pascal's. So the Visitors' Sunday had a three and a half year run and slowly faded away. The sharing program blossomed.

The School

One of the first decisions I had to make was to hire a new principal. I still had a lot to learn about this absolutely critical part of the pastor's role. After two years, I knew I had made a mistake. It was not as catastrophic as my first venture into this area, but less than stellar.

I gathered a really good committee to advise me on the next choice. We hit the jackpot and hired Dennis Wozniak, a fine educator with several years' experience in African American Catholic schools both as teacher and principal. Dennis had a great heart and a special love for the children in our community. He remained at St. Cyril School for the next fifteen years until it closed.

The school was one of our major contributions to the wellbeing of the community. Everybody felt proud of the good Catholic education the children were receiving. The school was one of the most hopeful ventures in the entire community. Under Dennis Wozniak's leadership, we strengthened the curriculum. We worked hard to get our graduates into Catholic High Schools which gave them the likelihood that they would attend college and have the surest ticket out of poverty. We worked equally hard to get other graduates into quality public schools.

Once again St. Anne's made a significant contribution. Several families gave substantial scholarship help to our graduates that allowed them to attend Catholic high schools. These sponsorships often included personal relationships between the families. It also led to the students getting summer jobs in various downtown offices which gave them a great exposure. We did not know it at the time, but it held the seeds of the revolutionary *Cristo Rey* model of education that is such a blessing for poor areas throughout the nation today.

Unexpected Guests

In the process of depopulation, several programs that found it almost impossible to locate in any other neighborhood moved quietly into the Woodlawn community. First on the list were halfway houses. There were several of them. They housed mental patients who had been released from institutions as a result of Reagan's budget cuts. The assumption was that all these people needed to do was to take their medicine. In fact, this was the beginning of the homeless problem that we have lived with since the early 80s.

The proprietors of the halfway house took the people off the street. In return the residents had to hand over their social security check. The owners gave them food, housing and a dollar a day for expenses. It was a difficult situation for these residents and not much better for the larger community.

Another new program involved a couple of buildings that housed intellectually challenged adults living in apartments. This project had on site case workers and generally was a good program but most families did not want to live next door to such a program. That is why it ended up in Woodlawn.

Next there was a detox center. This was closely monitored and beneficial to the community and the affected individuals.

Finally, there was a special nursing home that housed men and women suffering an escalating level of human deprivation as one ascended the eight floors of the residence. All the residents of these different locations had encounters with the parish.

Some of the halfway house residents came to the Sunday mass. Several came after taking their medicine and others without the medicine. The latter often became a minor disturbance as they talked and sang to the statues but generally were easily guided out if they were truly troublesome.

One of residents became my friend. Her name was June. She always came with her bike and tennis racket and distinct ankle high gym shoes out of the fifties. June was in her early sixties and a smoker. She always was "borrowing" money to buy her cigarettes because she said she was robbed at her residence. That was probably true. From time to time I insisted that June pay me back a token amount when her smoke account got too high. One time she had developed a huge debt. I cut off the money for a while. Before Mass, June was relentless that she needed cash for her cigarettes. I refused to give more cash. At Communion time June stood before me as I held the host in front of her and said, "The Body of Christ." June responded, "Don't you ever forgive and forget."

Carmelite Formation

With the arrival of Dave Blanchard and John Rivera, I began a career of directing Carmelite interns that continues today almost three decades later. In the intern experience the young Carmelites are invited usually to have two years of living in community and sharing in pastoral work. It is a rich experience and makes everything about their life, studies, and commitment more real.

In 1986, I had two interns, Carl Markelz and an Irish Carmelite guest, Frankie Nealis. Both were teaching at Mt. Carmel High School where Carl would become principal and president for fifteen years before becoming our provincial in 2011. Frankie was on loan from the Irish Province. He grew up in northern Dublin and was a childhood friend of Bono, the leader of the famous rock group U2. Like his famous friend Frankie had a spectacular singing voice.

One particular day all the community members had to go to Washington on a 36 hour turn-around trip for an important justice and peace meeting. Frankie had a firm commitment related to his teaching job at Mt. Carmel High School and had to stay home by himself. The timing could not have been worse.

That evening he heard someone in the hallway outside his room. He looked out and there were two men. One man had a knife and was coming at him from fifteen feet away. He quickly closed and locked his door. The intruder demanded that Frankie come out. He did not. All the while he was marking the very heavy wooden door with the knife. Frankie tried to call 911 but the phone was dead. Then he went to the window and started screaming for help but the street was empty. The two men quickly left. Frankie continued to call out from his window but had little luck. He stayed utterly terrified all night.

In the morning, he went to teach but was still so shocked, that the principal, Fr. Dave Dillon, noticed his condition and responded immediately. Dave got the story and went into action quickly. He had many contacts with the police department and he went right to the top.

We returned from D.C. at 2 PM to find the police all over our residence. Shortly after we arrived, there was a call for me from a currency exchange about a check to be cashed. The police went there and picked up our recently hired maintenance man. He was one of the two men outside of Frankie's room. He also was the son of a prominent family in the parish.

We learned that he had been robbing us in different ways for a month and a half to feed the cocaine habit of his girlfriend. The night before he had taken a series of checks from the back of the checkbook.

We pressed charges, and to my great surprise, the only concern of the family was whether we would let them continue as parishioners. We had no problem with that.

Frankie survived that fateful night and that prepared him for his next job. He left the Carmelites a few years later and went on to become an active member of a peace community in Northern Ireland where he met his wife.

Major and His Crew

We had a group of gay men in the parish. They were active parishioners and openly accepted by the parishioners. One of them, Mr. Major Lucas, was the recognized leader and spokesperson. At this particular historical period, this was a radical breakthrough in the usual patterns of society. The African American community was more tolerant of gays than the country as a whole. I was blessed to be part of the experience.

The story had a tragic ending however. This was shortly after the AIDS epidemic broke out. Most of these fine men died of this tragic disease before much was known about it.

The Story of Frances

The major nursing home in the parish was a very special place. The building was eight stories high and each floor became host to more extraordinary patients with increasingly indescribable distortions and pathological expressions of the human body. When you arrived at the top floors, you had to keep yourself from gasping because these distortions of the human body were challenging even to the professional caregivers.

There was a lady in the parish who had a very precious and special gift. She found deep joy in connecting with these hidden patients. Frances was the clerk at the corner dry cleaners and a Eucharistic minister in the parish. One Sunday she asked if she could join me in my visit to the nursing home.

Soon, I was caught up in a deeply moving experience as I saw Frances relate to all of these patients with the most tender and gracious touch. Even the nurses were stunned. As Michael Jordan was born to play basketball, Frances was totally and spectacularly gifted to bring a gentle human touch into the extremely isolated lives of these poor patients, most of whom had been too overwhelming for their families. It was a thing of beauty. Frances gladly took over the responsibility of ministering to these special people each Sunday. She continued for several years until her health made it impossible.

The Housing Project

In my last year and a half in the parish, we started a program to get families into housing cooperatives where they could each own their individual apartment in a given building. A dozen and a half families got their apartments as part of a cooperative that owned a building. Working in cooperation with each other and learning the very complex technicalities of the housing market was a struggle. Those who survived have been blessed with both good housing and the benefit of substantial growth in the value of the property as the gentrification began and continues to the present.

The Rookie

One of the social activities of the parish was to use the parish school bus to go to various sporting activities such as White Sox baseball games or Bulls basketball games. In 1985, the Bulls were offering a special group package to help with the poor attendance. We got group tickets in the upper, "nose bleed area" for just $5. We knew a bargain when we saw it. We went as a parish group three different times to see "The Rookie" who we all knew was going to be far beyond special someday. His name was Michael Jordan. There were never $5 tickets after his rookie season!

Conclusion

My years as pastor were blessed with good, and even great, people on the staff and wonderful, patient and loving parishioners. They accepted me with all my foibles and gifts. They taught me many things: to preach with heart, voice and body; to be comfortable as a product of my South Side Irish heritage; to be open to the beauties of the African American culture; to learn how to listen to the parishioners and, finally, to slow down and smell the roses.

I had been called to become director of our formation program at Whitefriars Hall in Washington. It was time for me to move on after twenty-five years in Woodlawn. It was not easy. I needed six weeks away before I could return and handle a farewell party. I was very apprehensive but it turned into a real love fest with all the trimmings. Almost to a person, the parishioners failed to mention all the great things I did, at least great in my mind. What they all did say was thanks for walking with them, thanks for being there, thanks for being part of their lives. It is not so easy to walk the path of the families of Woodlawn. In the end, that was what really counted for them, just being there, day in and day out, walking with the people in the struggle as they joined Jesus on the road to Jerusalem.

I had come to realize that my insights and my words and my preaching were, most often, ahead of my lived reality. The way I lived did not truly flow from my public expressions and many of my personal thoughts. The goal for me was to catch up with my words, to close the gap. As I experienced my farewell with the people and listened to them express their love and support for me, I came to understand something special. My role as a priest, my walking with them, was in great part, just giving them the words to comprehend the rich reality that was their life. They were often the opposite of me. Their reality, their lived experience was ahead of their words. They, too, were in the process of realizing through our mutual ministry to each other that in their lives God has *"been there all along."*

In my farewell ceremony at the parish, one of my friends, Oresa Gardner, was chosen to speak for the community. Here is part of the text of her message:

> "Thank you for being here to lead and guide and to teach us as a Christian community.
>
> Thank you for working hard to break down the barriers of hatred, racism, and injustices to our oppressed people in this community at the risk of being criticized by your family and friends.
>
> Thank you for marrying our children and baptizing our babies and children.
>
> Thank you for sharing a meal with us as you got to know each member of the community one by one.

> Thank you for comforting us in time of our sorrows and crying and praying with us; for burying our dead. Thank you for visiting our loved ones in prison and at the hospital.
>
> Silver and gold I have none but such as I have, I give to you. I give God's peace to you for your new assignment in Washington!"

A significant part of my psychic energy during this time as pastor was consumed dealing with the demon of alcohol. This kept hidden from me the fact that God was using my weakness to proclaim the Gospel of Jesus Christ. Through the power of this proclamation there was a transformation taking place that I did not see at the time. I soon would learn that this is true evangelization.

Some twenty-five years later, when I was celebrating my 50th anniversary as a priest, I opened my homily with this statement.

> "I have tried to follow the insights of Woody Allen and St. Teresa of Avila. Woody says 95 percent of life is just showing up. I have tried to be faithful to that declaration. St. Teresa says, in the end, the story of all our lives is about the mercy God."

Looking back, especially at these very fateful years at the parish, I can see more plainly what was not clear to me at the time: God has *been there all along!"*

10

Back to the Books Again

Transition

Early on in mid-June 1989, I had gone to D.C. for a few days to get information about the doctor of ministry program at Catholic University and to bring some of my things. I remember one event vividly. Everybody was out of the house on a Sunday afternoon and I went down to the TV room. I tried to get a channel using the Chicago numbers. I said, "O my God, I don't even know the TV channels. What am I getting myself into!"

I was a nervous wreck during my final weeks in Chicago. I was uprooting after twenty-five years. I was totally possessive about the parish. My successor, Dan O'Neil, whom I held in high regard, clearly intended to be his own man. I planned to be with him for a couple of weeks in transition. He felt a couple of hours were sufficient so I was off to D.C. two weeks early.

I remember driving out of Chicago and arriving at Indianapolis, 150 miles away. I pulled the car over to the side of the road and cried for an hour and a half. It really hurt and it would take a while before I realized how deep the pain was. I took a vacation on the Jersey shore at a Carmelite residence and reported to Whitefriars Hall in mid-August.

First Year Plan

The idea for my first year was to live in the community, participate in the activities of the formation program and work on the doctor of ministry degree. I was in regular dialogue with the director, Quinn Conners, and got a good feel for the upcoming job.

Very shortly I got into the rhythm of life and found it a delightful experience. Among my classes three were outstanding: spirituality and human development with Quinn, St. Teresa of Avila with Jack Welch and pastoral counseling with a Catholic University professor, Doug Morrison. I wrote a paper for each course. Each of the professors suggested I tighten the paper and have it published. I never did.

The major requirement for the doctor of ministry degree was to write a significant paper giving the foundation, explanation and plan for executing a pastoral project that would integrate the studies and lead to practical pastoral activities.

My chief concern was what kind of formation director I was going to be. The formation program had a manual with a clear job description but I had learned as a pastor that, once I have the basic idea of the manual, my inclination was to use it only when I had a serious conflict. I needed to be myself with my vision and my gifts.

Quinn had a doctorate in psychology. I was not going reject the many aspects of the program he brought to the table; in fact, I was going to implement them as best I could. Yet, I knew I had to be myself.

So in thinking about my paper and project, I asked who am I and what is my message?

These questions brought me to three major themes: the Carmelite identity, the justice perspective and spirituality. The more I thought about these ideas, I knew they were strong but something was missing.

I knew there were members of our province who were apprehensive about me in this job with the men of our future. They felt my approach was limited and only good for the inner city. In their view I was a one-tune guy.

This suspicion led me to think about my experience with the middle class parishes on justice and peace issues. It always seemed that only a small percentage, rarely higher than ten percent, were enthused about the issues flowing from justice and peace. I remember dealing with many parishioners who came to ask for help starting a justice and peace committee in their parish. As I got more experience in this struggle, I would ask them, "Do you have a committee on love in your parish?" They would always say, "Of course not, everything in the parish is about love."

I would then refer them to the iconic quote from the famous Synod on Justice:

> "Action on behalf justice and participation in the transformation of the world fully appear to us as a constitutive dimension of the preaching of the Gospel or, in other words, of the Church's mission for the redemption of the human race and its liberation from every oppressive situation."

I pointed out that justice concerns were totally integral to the most fundamental task of the parish, to preach the gospel. I said if they understood this, they would not need a special committee.

As I reflected on this, I came to the conclusion that the missing leg to my three-legged stool of Carmelite identity, the justice perspective and spirituality was the obvious one we all take for granted, evangelization.

As I researched materials on evangelization, I was blown away by how little was available at this time in the fall of 1989 as I researched the libraries at Catholic University and the Washington Theological Union. This surprise led me to go back to the original source on evangelization for our times, the encyclical of Pope Paul VI, *Evangeli Nuntiandi* (EN).This proved be an absolutely spectacular and mind-boggling experience.

I am very intuitive. I saw the basic outline of my paper and project. It was how evangelization, as understood in the papal document, brings together in a creative and unifying way the three major concerns of my life: Carmelite identity, the justice perspective, and spirituality.

The title of my paper was *"Evangelization in Carmelite Formation."* I was in the process of defining my tenure as director of formation. The integrating message of evangelization unifies the depth and connection of Carmelite identity, the justice perspective and spirituality. A major part of the paper would be the growth among the Carmelites in understanding their charism in the post -Vatican II days.

To evangelize is to touch someone's heart, mind, and imagination with the Risen Lord. The encounter becomes so significant that the person begins to reinterpret and redirect his or her whole life around Jesus. To evangelize is to help another person pay attention to, celebrate, and live in terms of the living God, revealed fully by Jesus and present in our human experiences.

Paul VI sees that evangelization is much more than one form of ministry of the Word. It includes all pastoral activity of the Church in the effort to give birth to a new age and a new world.

> "For the Church, evangelizing means bringing the Good News into all strata of humanity, and through its influence transforming humanity from within and making it new... The Church evangelizes when she seeks to convert, solely through the divine power of the message she proclaims, both the personal and collective consciences of people, the activities in which they engage, and the lives and concrete milieu which are theirs." (EN # 18)

In EN #15, Paul VI points out the reciprocal links between the Church and evangelization. EN states: "The Church is born of the evangelizing activity of Jesus and the Twelve... And it is above all his mission and his condition of being an evangelizer that she is called upon to continue."

It is the mission of evangelization, therefore, that has the Church, not the

Church that has the mission. So within the Church every ministry, whether it be pastoral care or explicitly missionary, whether outreach to the unchurched and inactive or dealing with the spiritual growth of the faithful, whether justice and peace concerns or family service – all ministries converge to serve the primary and essential mission of evangelization.

I was, indeed, going to be a one tune guy. The tune was going to be evangelization and it did not matter whether Carmelites were working in the inner city, at the high schools or in the middle class parishes. The task was simple and clear. We need to evangelize.

In EN #17, Paul VI continues to point out the depth of meaning of evangelization:

> "Any partial and fragmentary definition which attempts to render the reality of evangelization in all its richness, complexity and dynamism does so only at the risk of impoverishing it. It is impossible to grasp the concept of evangelization unless one tries to view all its essential elements."

Paul VI's understanding of evangelization then, is very grand indeed! It involves transformation of humanity and the whole world from within. So discipleship is a call to responsibility for the world, to bring the light and truth of Jesus into all its dimensions. To evangelize is to become instrumental in facilitating and continuing God's self-revelation to our world. Jesus, the fullness of God's self-disclosure, is the Message. It is much more than passing on doctrine, tradition, memorized passages from Scripture, or creating religious peak experiences.

In pointing out the essential content of evangelization in Chapter III, Paul VI brings into focus some basic elements that are too often overlooked:

> To evangelize is first of all to bear witness in a simple and direct way to God revealed by Jesus Christ in the Holy Spirit; to bear witness that in His Son, God has loved the world – that in his Incarnate Word he has given being to all things and has called all people to eternal life. (EN #26)

> Salvation in Jesus Christ is the central message. (EN #27)

> Evangelization is the interplay of the Gospel and concrete life.

> The Gospel frees from all dehumanizing forces in the world (EN #29).

> The Gospel brings liberation from sin (EN #36).

> Happiness is found in God, humankind's final goal (EN #35)

Paul VI then adds his insights into one of the most difficult theological concepts in the era after the Council, the nature of salvation. It is especially on this topic of salvation that the intimate connection between justice and peace and evangelization is clearly established. He elaborates the statement of the bishops in the synod on justice that justice is central to evangelization. His reflection shows a sense of balance and of openness. The meaning of salvation is a very fertile area of theological and pastoral creativity in recent times. *Evangeli Nuntiandi* has made an important contribution to the enrichment of the idea of salvation.

Evangeli Nuntiandi balances the traditional aspects of the spiritual and extra-historical idea of salvation with the newer concept of intra-historical liberation of all people, the area of justice and peace. The encyclical declares that there is "need to restate clearly the specifically religious finality of evangelization" (EN #32). Likewise, the liberation which *Evangeli Nuntiandi* proclaims "cannot be contained in the simple and restricted dimension of politics, economics, social or cultural life; it must envision the whole person… including one's openness to the absolute, even the divine absolute" (EN #33).

Paul VI is adamant in his insistence that salvation begins within history. He adds that the proclamation of the Good News demands a call for liberation from all that prevents our full humanity. "The Church…has the duty of assisting the birth of this liberation, of giving witness to it, of ensuring that it is complete. This is not foreign to evangelization" (EN # 30).

The language of the document often interchanges the words" salvation" and" liberation" or talks of "liberating salvation": "Between evangelization and human advancement – development and liberation – there are in fact profound links" (EN #31). Maintaining the creative tension, he repeats,

> "Nevertheless, the Church re-affirms the primacy of her spiritual vocation and refuses to replace the proclamation of the Kingdom by proclamation of forms of human liberation; she even states that her contribution to liberation is incomplete if she neglects to proclaim salvation in Jesus Christ" (EN #34).

The reign of God in Jesus, and conversion thereto, demands both ongoing and radical commitment to the transformation of individuals and social structures toward God's plan of justice and peace, love and full integrity for creation and all humankind.

Paul VI affirms that the Church believes that all temporal and political liberation, no matter how strong its claim of theological foundation, risks massive self-deception without authentic spirituality as its driving force.

"It carries with itself the germ of its own negation and fails to reach the ideal that it proposes for itself, whenever its profound motives are not those of justice in charity, whenever its zeal lacks a truly spiritual dimension and whenever its final goal is not salvation and happiness in God." (EN #35).

Pope John Paul II was thinking along the same lines. He went back to *Evangeli Nuntiandi* as the basis of his theme of "New Evangelization." His major encyclical on "New Evangelization" *Redemptio Missio* was issued in 1989. I only became familiar with *Redemptio Missio* much later but I had the same basic themes that the Polish Pope taught because *Evangeli Nuntiandi* was our common source. His teachings, unlike mine, however, brought evangelization into the mainstream of church practice and pastoral vision. Nowadays, everything is measured in terms of evangelization, but in 1989 I did not anticipate a difficult time interesting the students in my vision of the centrality of evangelization. Another of life's surprises awaited me.

The passionate excitement that I felt about evangelization was the result of a long journey. I started out with questions about passing on the "South Side Irish Tribal customs." Then I ran into the conflict with the concept of the servant Church and the *Chicago Plan*. Painfully I learned the need for prayer and spiritual depth in my crusading days. I learned that community organizing has to go beyond self-interest if it is going to be an expression of the Gospel. Next was my struggle to integrate my metaphors of the Doctor and the Monsignor as models of ministry. Then, the search to bring the justice perspective to the work with Call to Action came into play. In time I realized that I had used the word evangelization in my five years as pastor at St. Clara-St. Cyril, but now, with the leisure of study and reflection, I grasped how shallow my understanding had been compared to the wonders of Paul VI's vision laid out in *Evangeli Nuntiandi*.

Another marvelous insight blossomed as I studied *Evangeli Nuntiandi*. I knew something special had been happening in my years as pastor. The sense of community, the sense of unity, the sense of growth among the people was clear. However, there was something more.

It was simple enough but profound. *Evangeli Nuntiandi* pointed it out. The real gift of the Gospel, the liberation of the Gospel, always had to go beyond socio-economic progress. We always need to be aware that it is not spiritual or historical, not material or sacred. It is not either/or. Both are part of the transformation the Gospel wants to call forth but the balance is always very difficult to achieve. In fact, social-economic progress often times is the result of a paternalism that steals the dignity of the poor.

What I was able to understand, now, from a distance, was that the entire evangelization effort was bringing the people in touch with their dignity in a powerful way. In simple truth, the Gospel was working. When it works, there is a dignity and hope; there is transformation and commitment to remain faithful to the struggle. This is a beautiful thing. This was the reality I could not give a name to. The community was really walking with Jesus.

Paul VI's definition of evangelization is both profound and complex. It takes time to grow into it. It is worth repeating.

"For the Church, evangelizing means bringing the Good News into all strata of humanity, and through its influence transforming humanity from within and making it new... the Church evangelizes when she seeks to convert, solely through the divine power of the message she proclaims, both the personal and collective consciences of people, the activities in which they engage, and the lives and concrete milieu which are theirs. (EN #18)

11

Whitefriars Hall

In April 1990, we moved into a renovated Whitefriars Hall. The final stages of this $5 million project would linger on into the early fall. The job had accomplished a true transformation of the building built in 1940.

In June we were scheduled for our provincial chapter, a gathering of all the members of our Carmelite province to select leaders and set priorities. Quinn was the favorite to step up to be provincial. He won the election easily.

I stepped into a dual role. I was now director of formation and the prior or superior of the community. There were about 35 men in the community. They fell into the following four categories: permanent residents who were mostly professors and retired professors, students who were in vows and nearing the conclusion of their seven years of formation, newly arrived students who were being introduced to religious life and beginning their first year of theological studies, priests who were working on an academic degree or on a sabbatical year. Some were from foreign countries.

The basic formation program had four stages over a seven year period. The first was a year of introduction to religious life called the pre-novitiate year. This took place at Whitefriars. The students began their first year of theological studies.

The second stage was the novitiate. This year was dedicated to the study and practice of Carmelite life. It was free of any academic work and was aimed at introducing the men to a deeper spirituality and prayer life. At the end of this year the students made temporary vows of poverty, chastity, and obedience for three years.

The next phase was the intern program. During this time students were assigned to a Carmelite community, usually a parish or high school, and mentored as they ministered and lived the life of the community for two years.

Finally, the students arrived at Whitefriars for the final three years of theological studies at the Washington Theological Union (WTU). During this time the students made their final vows. At the end of third year most, but not all, chose to become deacons for six months and then were ordained.

Before coming to Whitefriars I already had a good deal of experience with the intern students over the years. I had often presented workshops for novices and many other workshops with the professed students. The pre-novices were new to me and I had a lot to learn about their experience.

From early May to the beginning of August I was settling into the new job. My great energy consumer, however, was the doctor of ministry paper. While I enjoyed the challenge it became increasingly an obstacle for me in doing my job.

During the second semester of my study year, sometime in March, my director, who was to guide me in my paper, suddenly left Catholic University. They never gave me an explanation or a replacement.

In October I turned in my paper. It was a pass/fail grade. I passed. However, the new person in charge now had a truckload of suggestions which basically meant re-writing the paper. I made a quick decision. The academic degree could wait to another lifetime but I would develop the workshop on my own. This proved to be a liberating decision and I was now free to plunge wholeheartedly into the formation activity.

Basic Program

The formation program aimed to give each student a sense of his responsibility to grow in human and Christian maturity and their Carmelite identity and to develop the intellectual and psychological skills necessary to be a public minister in the Church.

The house had a regular schedule of morning prayer, evening prayer, Eucharist, meals, and recreation. Every two weeks the students had a process called "group" in which six or seven of them would share their experience. This was led by a professional facilitator.

I was assisted by a member of the New York Province of Carmelites which had a few students in the program. Chris Howe and I divided the students between us and had a personal session with each student every two weeks. We called these "one-on-one" sessions. This particular time proved helpful in getting to know the students at a deeper level and to help them in very specific ways.

Probably the most important part of the program was the shared community life. This, by its very nature, brought its own challenges and opportunities for personal and spiritual growth.

Big Surprise

Most all new arrivals in the pre-novitiate year were in their late twenties or early thirties or beyond. These were men who had some life experience. They had gone through a personal discerning process to initiate a contact with the Carmelites. Then they had, at the minimum, several months of a joint discerning period with a Carmelite vocation director which included a retreat with other candidates. They had independent psychological testing and an interview with the regional superior and the director of formation. Besides all of this, they went through a substantial uprooting including leaving a job, family and friends. All of this together was no small investment.

My surprise was how many of the first year students were still very ambivalent about any serious commitment. Many were far from ready to put their nickel down. Their uncertainty called for a serious adjustment on my part.

It became evident very early that these first year students needed a lot of attention. They were hit with many serious challenges all at once. They were in a new religious and academic environment. They were meeting new companions. They were beginning the study of theology that shattered many of their intellectual assumptions and prejudices. Now they had to live in community to share time, space, and personal conveniences at an unprecedented level.

Shortly after I left the job of director of formation, the province determined it would be more beneficial to separate this first year, the pre-novitiate year, from Whitefriars Hall. It was a wise and prudent decision.

Crisis Management

These first four or five months offered a filtering process which the students either began a healthy adjustment process or some real problems surfaced. The following examples are from the four years of my tenure.

One young man was entranced with my story of ministry with the poor and justice and peace. He was anxious to sit down with me. After several inexplicable cancellations for this appointment, he disappeared one weekend. I soon learned why. He was in his room on a binge. He was a binge drinker and the pressure caught up with him. He was on the next bus home.

On another occasion, the police from suburban Virginia interrupted my lunch with a request for a conference. This one proved to be a whopper. The case began with a report of some damaged property which was the concern of the police but it played itself out as a potential public scandal and eventually blackmail. With quick action guided by our lawyers we avoided a serious problem for the Carmelites and the archdiocese. The next morning while I was driving the confused individual to the train station, he asked if I would write a letter of recommendation for him to another seminary.

We had a case of a kleptomaniac. Such a character can wreak havoc in a community. This one was caught up in his pathology, became careless, and was caught. He too was expelled.

There were the lesser cases of a student who felt all the teachers at WTU were heretics and a young man who was inflicting bodily harm to himself because of his distorted sense of his sinfulness.

These men were the exception and their incompatibility surfaced soon enough. However, the purpose of the formation program was to determine whether these men had the basic human maturity needed to grow in Christian maturity directed by the Carmelite tradition and spirituality. It was a seven year program that had several check points along the way.

Disappointment

As I got into the rhythm of the first year I became comfortable in my role. In spite of a few crisis situations, I felt there was a positive and warm atmosphere in the community. I was able to pay special attention to the pre-novitiate students as most were making a positive adjustment in a difficult and challenging situation.

Slowly, however, I began to realize that I was not doing what I truly wanted to do. I wanted to influence the students with a vision and message of evangelization with all the rich pastoral consequences for future leaders. I could not find space and time to implement my vision.

The dominant reality for all students was the academic program of WTU. The Union, as it was often called, was a fine and progressive educational program. Its main thrust was to prepare ministers. Our students received an excellent education at the Union. Two of the best professors at the Union, Jack Welch in spirituality and Donald Buggert in systematic theology, lived in the house and shared time meals with the students.

However, for me, it was a paradox. The WTU program took all their time and energy. I slowly realized that what was left was the psychological part of the program that Quinn had put in place. I saw that this component was extremely important. However, over the next four years, the lack of a pastoral concern in formation in the house became more and more problematic for me.

Another disappointment was that the house had little connection to the city and to the poor. My efforts to develop something in this area, once again, proved unrealistic given that time and energy after WTU's program.

The Hispanics Arrive

The province had an active Hispanic ministry commission. One of their projects was vocations. In my second year, 1991, four young men from Mexico with minimal English skills arrived early in the summer. After an intense two months of English studies, they began to take a few classes at WTU along with further English classes.

Their presence in the community was both a gift and a challenge. They brought a lively and youthful enthusiasm and a new culture. Some in the community had difficulty adjusting to their presence. At the same time we failed to make enough adjustment in the program to ease them into the process with more time and support for the long cultural journey we were demanding of them. Eventually, three of the more than twenty students became ordained for different dioceses.

Outside Ministry

Once I was settled into the routine of the house, I felt a need for some form of personal ministry outside the house. I made a connection with two parishes that were going to be a wonderful part of my life. The first was a suburban parish, St. Rose of Lima, in Gaithersburg, MD. I assisted at masses each weekend and eventually became involved in adult faith formation through programs, workshops, and retreats. In time, I even considered becoming a part-time associate pastor.

The other assignment was in a very dynamic African American parish in southeast Washington, D.C. The parish recently had had a major crisis when its pastor, George Stallings, left to form a new church with himself as bishop.

The new pastor was an incredible priest, Monsignor Ray East. He was nationally famous as a preacher and a great spokesperson for the African American Catholic community. He was gifted and energized in many special ways. I learned a great deal about ministering to the Catholic African American community from him.

The parish was named St. Teresa of Avila. The parish had two masses, one at 7:30 AM and the other at 11 AM with the usual length of the service two and a half to three hours. Even Ray East, the original energizer bunny, was hard pressed to do a six hour liturgical marathon every Sunday morning.

I felt privileged to share the journey with these folks. I was the beneficiary of their encouragement to develop my skills in the awesome and beautiful tradition of African American preaching.

Sister Angele

Late in the first year it became apparent to me that some of the young men were challenged by the role of women at WTU and in the Church in general. I responded by recruiting a special person to join our formation team. I hired Sr. Angele Sadlier, O. Carm. Angele was a mature and experienced Carmelite nun who was a member of the Carmelite Sisters from New Orleans.

Angele brought a bundle of gifts to the formation program. The most important gift was a loving patience in accepting the young men as they were. Some of the students, and a few of the other priests in the house, had trouble with idea of a woman being on the formation team. I saw it as a marvelous bequest to all of us.

Liturgy

One area that I enjoyed very much was the liturgy. We hired a professional liturgist to help with our worship services. They were beautiful and inspiring. I found an outlet for my desires for a more pastoral program in my homilies which were well received.

All the students received a good hands–on education in liturgy through the daily celebration of the Eucharist. Likewise, we were always gifted with good voices and most of the time with good musicians.

Evangelization Workshop

As we began to get ready for the second year, I made a few changes. First of all, I brought the pre-novices in four weeks early. Now, with Angele joining Chris Howe and me, we had time to pay more attention to the new students. It also gave them time to get to know one another and to become more familiar with the city.

The next change was a major one. I brought all the students in the formation program back to Whitefriars for a weekend workshop on evangelization. This student gathering, which included the novices and interns, was something completely new and proved to be a good experience at many levels. It has continued annually ever since.

I sent each student a brief sheet with a few items I wanted them to consider in preparation for the weekend.

I want to ask you to do a brief preparation for the workshop on Evangelization this weekend.

1. I would like you to reflect on yourself as a minister, religious and priest (for the ordination candidates). What do you want to be in this area? How will you look in the future? Try to get as concrete as possible. List at least five major characteristics of the type of religious person you hope to become. Be as specific as your heart, mind, and imagination will free you to be in drawing this portrait. Then give consideration to what you perceive to be the major obstacles for you on this road. Be ready to share as much as you want to on this topic.

2. Give some time to the following questions and be ready to share your observations:

A- What is the Good News for you?

B- How do you experience the Good News?

C- How do you respond to the Good News?

D- How do you share and proclaim the Good News?

E- How does your response to the above tie into the purpose of your life?

3. I am inclosing a few sheets for you to read. Numbers 17, 18, and 19 are three central paragraphs from *Evangeli Nuntiandi* (Evangelization in the Modern World). This 1976 document of Paul VI is still the major Church statement on evangelization.

The concepts of *Evangeli Nuntiandi* were new to the students. Some grasped the depth of the message and others were not ready yet. Perhaps, they needed to hear it from Pope John Paul II.

During the workshop the one presentation that did stir the interest of all was my conference on celibacy. This generated a lot of discussion. Most participants liked the fact that I laid out a picture that was concrete and practical while at the same time putting the entire message into a spiritual context that set a high ideal.

A Wonderful Opportunity

In 1991 I was invited to become a member of the Order's international commission on justice and peace. My commitment to this project eventually filled out a full decade. This was a special event in my life. I had a chance to meet some talented and inspiring Carmelites from around the world. I was able to travel and see Carmelite life in many different places and in different styles. The commission basically met every two years. During this time I went to Rome twice, Madrid, Holland, and Zimbabwe and I hosted one meeting in Los Angeles.

The Carmelites had been upgrading their vision ever since all religious orders were called by Vatican II to return to their original charism. This process involved a series of regular international gatherings of the superiors and selected members. This justice and peace commission played a significant role in gathering the relevant justice and peace elements of this renewal. Our proposals were then presented to the general chapter in 1995 that developed a new set of constitutions that were progressive in many areas especially in spirituality, justice, and peace. I was happy to have played a small role in this progress.

During my time on this Commission, I remember three personal encounters that were exceptional. The first was in 1994 in Zimbabwe. Our meeting was immediately after a gathering of all the Carmelites in Africa. One of these men was Robbie MacCabe. He was an Irish Carmelite who broke the mold in many ways. As a young man he was an exceptional amateur tennis player who competed at Wimbledon.

He had a life threatening condition as a young man. He had tuberculosis. He promised to become a priest if he survived. He recovered but went onto medical school and eventually became a world renowned specialist in tropical diseases. Only after four years as a doctor did he finally decide to join the Carmelites. Soon he left for the missions in Rhodesia.

A revolutionary war followed shortly after his arrival. He was kicked out of the country for treating the wounded rebel soldiers. He ended up in Kenya where he developed a distinctive style of ministry.

Fr. MacCabe had a van and travelled with a migrant tribe as their doctor and their priest for most of the year. Then often he returned to Dublin to lecture on tropical diseases. He received several honorary degrees and other special recognition for his medical contributions.

I was able to spend the better part of a day with Fr. MacCabe as we visited a number of mission bases in the countryside. At each of these bases there was a small medical facility, a little more than a hut with beds. The Irishman was like a kid in a candy store in his exuberant joy and excitement of how wonderful these primitive facilities were. He told us his biggest problem was cleanliness because his migrant people stayed greased over the entire body all the time to protect themselves from the heat of the tropical sun in the day and the cold of the desert at night. For him, clean sheets on the bed were a wildly extravagant luxury.

We had a group of six that travelled together the whole day. One of the members was a beautiful young Dutch doctor who was finishing special studies in tropical medicine. She was thrilled to make the connection with Fr. MacCabe. She acted as if she were spending a day with Martin Luther King. It was not much different for me. It was a very special experience being in the presence of such a truly authentic and humble servant of the Gospel.

Fr. MacCabe stayed with his beloved migrant parishioners from 1977 to a month before his death in 2011.

The second encounter was meeting Fr. Carlos Mesters. While Leo Mahon has been credited with initiating the base communities in Latin America, Carlos, a Carmelite Scripture scholar from Brazil, is the person who made the Bible come alive for the base communities in Latin America. He is renowned throughout the continent as the Scripture scholar of the poor. Carlos' presentation on Elijah at the 1983 general chapter of the Carmelites was a major event in Carmelite renewal. Carlos gave a clear insight into the connection of spirituality and justice in the story of Elijah. He presented an image of Elijah that was challenging and inviting. It was a major contribution to Carmelite self-understanding in the following decades.[9]

I was with Carlos for six of my ten years on the Commission. It was a fortunate time for me when I was in his presence.

Finally, my third encounter was of a very different nature. In 1993, after a meeting in Rome, I decided to take five days to visit Ireland for the first time.

I spent three days with the Carmelites in Dublin. The city was a true wonderland for me. I noticed all these people carrying little phones. At the time I was only familiar with the large phones some few people had in their cars. The Irish were far ahead of us in the cell phone world.

But the encounter came when I went to visit some relatives in my parents' home town of Kilarney in County Kerry.

My mother's sister had married my father's brother. John O'Sullivan, one of the sons of this union, was very close on the DNA chart. I was amazed how he looked just like my father. Then he started to tell stories of my father whom he knew well because my father had visited Ireland eight times between 1948 and 1970. Finally, as we went on a drive around the lakes of Kilarney, he gave me a jab in the ribs after a joke just like my father often did. The whole day was a surreal experience as if I had been able to be with my father for one special day.

Puerto Rican Syndrome

In my first year and half at St. Clara during my first assignment, there were a lot of Puerto Rican families. I noticed something about many of the fathers of these families. They were in Chicago for only one reason. They needed the job to take care of their family and they headed back to their native island as soon as a job opened up for them. They had no emotional investment in Chicago.

That experience was easy for me to identify because that was my father's story. I was soon to find out it struck closer to home than even that familial connection.

As the years passed at Whitefiriars, I was experiencing uneasiness. I could not put a finger on it. I wanted to return to work with the poor but I understood two things about my situation at Whitefriars. I had made a commitment for six years and I intended to fulfill that promise. Secondly, I knew this was an important work that transcended my personal feeling.

Eventually I shared these feelings of unrest with Quinn. Likewise, when my friend and guide, Ernie Larkin visited, I shared my story with him. He suggested that I take my concerns to prayer with a totally open mind. He said to just sit in silence and listen. Do not have an agenda for God. This I did for at least several days. Soon I was surprised about what surfaced in my consciousness. I slowly realized that I never truly mourned my departure from Chicago.

I began a process of mourning and I let the hurt come into the open. It was painful but healthy. I saw that I was a victim of the Puerto Rican Syndrome like my father. Down deep, I was passing time till I returned to Chicago. Once this was out in the open, I was free to address it and accept my situation with new freedom. I became comfortable down deep for the first time in a good while.

Then the God of surprises had another of his special deliveries for me. Sometime after this process, I cannot tell you if it was a week, or several months, Quinn came to my door and asked if I would consider going to St. Raphael in LA. If I had not gone through the liberating process of both mourning and finally truly leaving Chicago, I would have come up with countless reasons why I could not go to LA. The reasons did not come and I will soon begin my twentieth year in an assignment that has been a spectacular gift from God. As I like to say, God has *been there all along.*

12

St. Raphael: The Early Years

Setting the Scene

Before I arrived in Los Angeles I hired Jaime Morales who was working on a Carmelite project with Hispanics. He would be my assistant. This was a particularly important while I worked on my Spanish the first several months. I knew nobody else in the parish and very few in the city. All that would change rapidly.

I would find the situation in the parish challenging. The situation in the school was frightening. The situation in the neighborhood was exciting, bewildering, and an invitation to test my urban studies' skills.

I soon found that there was $40,000 in the bank for the parish and about $1.5 million in maintenance repairs and upgrades necessary for the parish and school. There were few programs or activities in the parish. The liturgy had minimal participation. There was one English choir and no Hispanic choirs. There was no secretary, no cook, and no maintenance man. The final straw was when the outgoing pastor, Fr. Bill Smith, showed me how to count the collection and where to do the grocery shopping.

The situation in the school was so bad that after three months I went to the archdiocese to inquire about the proper procedure for closing the school. One example of the depth of the problem was that I had to ask seven upper grade students to leave the school in the first five months. Their behavior was devastating to the educational program in the school.

I had come to the parish to minister in the African American Catholic community. I felt God had blessed me with both the skill and the experience that few priests had in this area. I wanted to put these gifts to good use.

I soon learned that the neighborhood was in the process of rapid change. The African Americans, especially the lower middle class group that the parish served, were leaving. The Hispanics were arriving in great numbers. I would learn that in the northeast area of the parish, many families shared apartments. One family slept during the day and another family during the night. All the schools were trying to address the gross overcrowding by a year round schedule. The schools in our area remained heavily overcrowded in spite of this effort. But I had no problem facing the challenge of learning how to minister in the Hispanic community. While I had a basic grasp of the language twenty-five years earlier, my Spanish skills were all gone. I was essentially starting over with my Spanish at the age of 58.

The 77th Street Police District covers a large part of South Central Los Angeles. The murder rate is a fairly good barometer of the overall crime rate. In the six years (1989-1994) before I came to St. Raphael the average murder rate was 136 per year. With the changing population, the fact that the more violent Hispanic gangs were in another part of the city and better police work, the murder rate for my first six years (1995-2000) was 63 per year. As the population decreased with the change in the economy, my last six years (2007-2012) revealed an even more drastic drop in the murder rate, 41 per year.

Parish Staff

My first effort was to seek a parish secretary. Soon a volunteer showed up at the front door and solved the problem. Esther Manriquez had a long history in the parish. My predecessor, Fr. Bill Smith, would have nothing to do with her but the three previous pastors before him had all depended on her considerable secretarial skills. Soon Esther had us on the road to a well organized parish office.

Esther had an encyclopedic knowledge of the parish, a personality that was driven. She was not bashful about conflict if things did not go her way. She was ready for a twelve hour working day to prove her point. She was delighted to be back in the saddle again and was helpful in bringing me up to date with parish traditions, practices, and culture. Her incredible energy betrayed her age in the early seventies.

I did not have as much luck with developing a parish staff. I ended up going down three or four dead end roads. I had to chalk it up as a learning experience. I depended on Esther while I was trying to develop a parish council and a school board. This was difficult because the people of the parish had no tradition or experience in meaningful lay participation in the parish and school. Eventually, patience paid dividends in this area.

Resurrection Babies

My actual introduction to the real life of the parish came from three events in the first several months. I call it the story of my three resurrection babies.

The first event happened on the second Saturday evening that I was in the parish. There were all kinds of police sirens passing the rectory. I looked out and saw that the squad cars had stopped just down the street. I went to check out the scene.

An eleven year old boy had been playing with a gun with his two cousins. He ended up with a bullet right in the center of his forehead. He looked like he was asleep with this small red ring on his forehead. After the anointing, the police asked that I go to the station with the parents because, according to California law, they were to be charged with the crime. It proved to be an even more traumatic evening. Finally, the parents were freed when the uncle admitted that the gun was his. A few days later a caravan of vans left for the funeral in Mexico.

After some weeks, I saw the mother before Mass with this glorious glow on her face. I soon learned why. While in Mexico, her cousin, the mother of a large family, gave birth to a baby girl. She gave the new born child to the sorrowing mother because of the poverty of her large family. I was delighted to be able to bless the child that morning before Mass.

The second story was the death of a two year old whose head was crushed by a falling bookcase. After twelve weeks, with the mother in round-the-clock watch in the trauma center, the child died. The funeral was the first time I preached in Spanish.

One year later, on the first anniversary of that child's death, we were again gathered in the church to baptize the family's newborn son. These two families left the parish after a few years.

The third story was about a graduate of our school who was a sophomore at Verbum Dei High. He was one of five killed at a Quincianera party by an insanely jealous husband who shot wildly into a crowd. Nine months later we baptized the family's newborn child. She now works at the rectory and is planning to study bio-medical engineering when she graduates from St. Mary High next year.

My three resurrection babies were an early introduction into the life and hope that are such a powerful presence for the people in the midst of the pain and loss that are such a prevalent part of South Central Los Angeles.

Gang Funeral

One way I began to learn about the neighborhood was by walking the streets. I was often told to be careful about one or other block because of the gangs. That made me more desirous of walking that way. I needed to learn and get connected.

The neighborhood has more than its share of dysfunctional families. However, the great majority of folks are trying to raise their kids as best they can. I have come to feel deeply the fear and challenge that parents have in living on the edge of violence. This is one of the most complicated features of our neighborhood: raising children in this threatening environment.

One night on a Larry King show about gangs in LA, I heard statistics that go right to the heart of any parents' anxiety. Connie Rice, a renowned civil rights lawyer and an outstanding spokesperson on the gang problem, gave these stats. The odds of dying by a terrorist attack in the US are 1 in 800,000. The odds of being murdered in West LA, a more affluent neighborhood less than fifteen miles and two galaxies away, are 1 in 78,000. The odds of being murdered in South LA are 1 in 2,000. Parents in our community may not know the numbers but the reality is in the deep recesses of their hearts, 24/7. They develop a lifestyle and strategies to survive and to have their children live as normal as possible in this painful context.

The gangs are a source of violence and conflict in a small group but the majority suffers the various degrees of consequences from this violence and conflict.

"The Bread Thing"

In my early days I had several funerals for gang members. I remember one in particular. I had forgotten part of it. In a surprising turn of events I received a letter, via Fr. Dave Blanchard, my Carmelite friend in El Salvador. A new employee of his somehow mentioned Fr. Tracy. She had been an acolyte for me the day of that particular funeral Mass in 1996. This is her poignant memory of the Mass that she recalled several years later.

> It was a funeral for a young teenager, a victim of gang violence. The church was totally filled and most of those in attendance were teenagers. I remember the gang members had written on their sweaters, "Liv till I Die".

> Fr. Tracy started speaking in a way I had never heard before. He started telling the youth that the length of their lives was not a decision for others to make, that their life had no price even for gangs, that they had to decision to make: to live for a long time out of the gang or to live for a short time in the gang. The gang members were angry and almost all of them who were present rose from their seats feeling a great disagreement.

> Immediately, Fr. Tracy told them to sit down out of respect for the family of the deceased. It was the longest Mass that I had ever attended. You could feel that atmosphere of tension and see in their eyes, their anger, pain, and rage.

After the funeral, Fr. Tracy immediately turned to us and told us to keep together as closely as we could. Within minutes, everyone had left the church; you could feel an odd atmosphere and especially the tension in Fr. Tracy.

St. Raphael always tried to help the young people of the community, helping them in their studies and with guidance and counseling. It is a tough job, since most start their involvement with gangs when they are in elementary school. Fr. Tracy loved to talk to the parents reminding them of the precious time they need to spend with their children. He always put the responsibility on the parents, since they arrived in the US to give their lives working and paying nannies to take care of their children.

It is a passion that Fr. Tracy and St. Raphael have and will always have to help the youth of the community.

A short time after graduating from St. Raphael School, Ruby Benitez, at age 15, moved to El Salvador because of her father's health concerns. After high school she attended the National University and earned a decree as an agricultural engineer. Fr. Dave Blanchard hired her to direct his many agricultural projects that assist and uplife the poor in farming ventures.

I remember well another part of that day. Several of the gang members were upset enough that they reached out for help. In the afternoon they took my suggestion, and came to confession. I remember telling one of them that he should go to Mass and receive Holy Communion. He said, "What is that? Is that the bread thing?" I felt the pain of how far we have to go and the joy of how we need to continue being faithful to proclaiming Jesus Christ as Lord and Savior.

The major way in which a parish like St. Raphael is different is how the social structures scream out to the people: "You are poor; you are inferior; you are the problem; you need to be different. Your color is your problem. Your language is your problem." The message is loud and clear: poor schools, poor housing, racial isolation, routine violence, prostitution, and drugs.

Against all these negative factors there is the call to one fundamental ministry that is pervades all we do – it is the ministry of giving people hope. We proclaim a God who is present and loving in the midst of chaos. Everything we do is committed to proclaiming and witnessing to a Gospel message that declares the gift of life in our midst, and says the last word is not death in the streets nor the life destroying power of drugs but the courage of struggling parents, hopeful young people, and joyful children all searching for love.

We will never have a complete solution to the problems of violence and poverty, of drugs, and dropouts. But in the midst of this darkness, we can be about "the Bread thing," and preach a Jesus who says life is not only possible but is a real option in any situation. More than anything else, "the Bread thing" is about a sacramental ministry. It is about being a sign of a deeper reality that gives hope for new life and new possibilities. "The Bread thing" is a call to stay in the struggle to make the changes that fight poverty and violence, that light the candle that guides us to a new day.

When I was a young priest the challenge of the gangs drew me to the streets to fix the problem. Now I knew that gathering and nourishing a faith community around the Eucharist was the most effective response. All the theory of my studies on evangelization was now concrete and real. Likewise, I came to a quick change of mind about closing the school and made up my mind to invest myself completely to save it. After the experience of the funeral that I came to call "the Bread thing," my agenda was clear. It was to gather the people, tell the story, and break the bread.

Two Other Funerals

There were two other funerals that were very significant for me in learning the complex reality of my new neighborhood, South Central Los Angeles.

The first was a story of Amparo.

One day before one of my bible study sessions, we were waiting for a few late arrivals. I noticed three people who lived just a half block from Florence and Normandie which was the epicenter of the 1992 civil unrest or riot depending on your point of view. This intersection is right in the center of our parish. I asked them about their experience that momentous weekend. Right away they told me a story of their mothers and grandmother. The lead individual was Amparo, a truly interesting character and a woman of faith. After the first night of the disturbance, at a time when the police had still abandoned the area, Amparo was going to the 8 AM Mass. As she came out of her house, a young neighbor she had known since he was in diapers, told her to get back in the house. He said it was too dangerous out on the streets. Amparo would have none of it. She said God would take care of her. She walked down the street to get to her daily Mass companions: a 70 year old friend and her 90 year old mother. After arguing some more, the young man gave in. He decided he would walk with them to St. Raphael, four blocks away, to keep them safe from any trouble. So he did. He also waited for them and walked them home.

What makes the story ironic was that this young man was Damien Williams. Shortly, he would become a *cause célèbre* for the wrong reason. He would be charged with bashing the head of Reginald Denny the night before not only on national TV but on world TV. This horrific sight became ingrained in the national consciousness. He would be charged and, ultimately, convicted of a lesser charge.

Truly good stories always draw us into the deeper mysteries of life, the struggle of sin and grace, the majesty and depravity of the human condition. Amparo's goodness brought out the goodness in Damien Williams at a time when he epitomized senseless violence for an entire nation. This is what the Church should be about: testifying to the truth by bringing light into the darkness.

In her own way Amparo preached the Gospel day in and day out. She was a very gregarious person who had a good word for everyone in the neighborhood. She did not realize it at the time but she was in more danger than from the violence on the streets that fateful morning. A few years later at the 8 AM Mass, she became disoriented. Within a short time she died of a cancerous tumor in the brain. Her death was an act of beauty as was her life. Her life had spoken the Gospel to the people who recognized the truth when they saw it. Her funeral filled the church completely and most of the visitors were African American neighbors of other denominations who saw in their Hispanic neighbor the beauty of the Gospel.

Priest of the People

Fr. Juan Izabal was the associate pastor when I arrived. Juan was a character always full of surprises. He was the second Hispanic priest in our Carmelite province and was terribly misunderstood by the majority of our members. Here is one of a hundred stories that led to this bad reputation.

Juan was scheduled to celebrate a wedding at 10 AM. He did not show. Another priest celebrated the Mass. As the couple was processing out, the priest saw Juan driving a rental truck down the street.

Juan was not a good communicator in any situation but especially when he was under pressure. Consequently, he lived with the label of being irresponsible. In fact, he was helping an undocumented family that had been put out on the street and in danger of losing all their things because they had no driver's license. Juan came to the rescue. He was confident that one of the four other priests in the house would cover the wedding. Multiply that event many times over and you can understand the source of Juan's reputation.

It was a totally different story in the Hispanic community where Juan was always on call in every emergency and always in tune with the beauty and idiosyncrasies of the culture.

When Juan died of throat cancer on January 31, 1996, we had his body available for viewing for three days. There was a constant stream of people. Finally, when we had the Mass of the Resurrection on Sunday afternoon, we had a sound system set up outside the church to handle the overflow. Even that was terribly inadequate. The police had to come to direct traffic away from the church because there just was no more space available.

After three months at our staff meetings, I realized Juan had no idea of what we were trying to do as a parish. I told him to forget the staff meetings and just take care of the Masses and baptisms and continue his work outside the parish. He was like a child on Christmas caught up in unbelief at such a wonderful gift. I encouraged him to just keep working with the people in his own special way.

Juan's parish was the entire Hispanic community. He was available for whatever the people needed and especially how the people needed it in the richness of their culture and traditions. Juan was of the people and for the people in a spectacular way. That is why the police had to come to turn the crowd away.

13

Gathering the Community

Eucharist: Source and Summit

Very early in my stay at St. Raphael it was clear that liturgy was the first major pastoral task. Vatican II taught that the Eucharist is "the source and summit of our Christian faith." (*Lumen Gentium #11*). Christian spirituality *is a two way street*. It leads *us from the Eucharist as a starting point into the world of our* daily life and it takes us back home to the Eucharist after our sojourn in the world needs new strength.

The bad news was few people were involved in any way in the liturgy. Only a few had minimal training in liturgical ministries. The good news was that we had an open field. The truth was the people were hungry for something new in this area.

Very quickly, Harry Wiley and his wife Gloria, long time parishioners, surfaced as trained liturgists. At this stage of his life, Harry was difficult to work with but he was open to growth and he brought many talents and gifts to the table. He proved to be a very positive factor after all was said and done.

A cultural conflict was inevitable given the history, ethnic makeup and the changing composition of the population: the majority moving rapidly from Black to Hispanic. Harry and Jaime Morales, my assistant, had many roles but cultural warriors soon surfaced as front and center for them as we began to work on liturgy. They became strong advocates for the African American and Hispanic cultural interests.

All throughout South Central Los Angeles, Blacks and Hispanics lived in tension with each other. Blacks were diminishing in numbers but were sophisticated politically. Hispanics had a long way to go politically but they had numbers which continued to grow with jaw-dropping speed. The Black and Brown clash was on.

Some of the conversations I heard from the Black community in the parish sounded exactly like the talk of my youth among white racists on the South Side of Chicago. Only this time, the Hispanics were the object of the racism. Nor were the Hispanics walking with the angels in their conversation about the Blacks.

I was determined to take this issue head on in the parish. It was a basic Gospel challenge. No institutions addressed it and few programs aimed at developing a reasonable dialogue. I felt the Church had to lead the way in this desert of isolation and tension.

An old Baptist minister told me that the devil comes into the church through the choir. I think the devil's favorite path of entry for Catholics is in the planning for the liturgy.

As we worked on the liturgy we made a great deal of progress. We had large numbers of people willing to be trained in all the liturgical ministries. We did this at the entry level in the parish, those entering liturgical ministry for the first time. Soon we began to take advantage of the rich resources of the archdiocese such as conferences, workshops and even extended certificate programs in this area for those who wanted a deeper level of training.

In short order we had several new choirs. Jaime's love for music became a driving force in this area. He would make his greatest contribution after he left the parish.

After six months we had a complete transformation of the liturgy from the previous decades and almost everyone was happy with the Sunday morning experience. However, culture soon impeded progress. An early example of the conflict was the liturgy committee's implementing of the Church's law that flowers should not be in the worship space during Lent. Most Hispanics felt this was the work of the devil. Not being able to bring roses to the Virgin was insane in their view. There were innumerable instances of this cultural conflict surfaced over the years. Gradually, they became less shrill and adjustment gradually less painful and more reasonable.

Popular religious practices also created cultural tensions between Hispanics and Blacks. My clear goal was to support these expressions of the faith known as popular religiosity and let the liturgy committee back off as much as possible.

My posture as pastor was to give maximum support to all popular religiosity and, at the same time, try to form everyone with a deep love and respect for the Eucharist and all liturgy. This "both/and" approach avoided a load of cultural conflict but conflict still remained.

On the positive side we made a commitment to celebrate as many of the expressions of the cultures as possible. We celebrated a program for Black

History Month which included a performance on this theme for the entire school. We did the same for Hispanic Awareness month. Then we had special days for the various nations such as Mexico, El Salvador, Guatemala, Belize and special days for the African Americans. St. Patrick did not make the calendar however!

My job was to keep the communications flowing. We had plenty of conflict and most of it resulted in growth. Jaime and Harry both benefitted from the expanded cultural horizons as the result of their cultural battles. The entire parish community benefited from their growth and adjustment.

Here Comes Maria

After my second year, Manny Ramirez, a long time director of religious education, left the program. A great number of people came with a message. In a strong and clear voice they pleaded for me to hire Maria Moran for the job.

I talked to Maria and was touched by her response. We offered her a full time job with a significant increase in salary. Yet she had to think about it because she would have to leave a family that she had been working with as a cleaning lady for 17 years.

She did decide to take the job and we have been blessed in so many ways ever since. Among her many gifts, Maria is generous to a fault with her time. She almost always is the last person to leave as we clean up after any parish event.

Maria immediately began a program of studies to become a master catechist. Her studies took more than three years. She also encouraged several of the catechists to get credentials from a wide range of programs available at the archdiocese.

In the meanwhile, because she was now full time, she was able to greatly expand the program. In two years there was a tenfold increase in the number of children participating in religious education.

The Matter of the Purse

A few months after my arrival at St. Raphael, I had a growing wish list. At the top of the list was a nun to work with the Hispanic community. Through the encouragement of a Carmelite friend of mine, I learned that a sister wanted to visit us as a possible site for her community's ministry.

So one evening in January 1995, I went to Los Angeles airport to pick up

Sister Isabel, a Carmelite sister from Houston. To my surprise, she had a companion. I had prepared the one guest room in the rectory, so with a quick shuffle, I placed the two nuns in rooms in the old convent, now a multi-purpose building. This was late Friday night. The plan was for the sisters to interview several groups in the parish, to participate in the liturgies and leave early on Sunday afternoon.

Right after the 8 AM Mass on Saturday, Sr. Isabel came up to me, a bit sheepishly, and said her purse was missing. I said, "Let's go look for it." We did and it was still missing. She had left it at the foot of her bed. Then I suddenly realized what she knew all along. Someone had come into her room in the middle of the night and stolen the purse. I was flooded with two strong emotions. "Thank you, Jesus, they were not harmed!" and "Goodbye, sisters. I can't blame you." Sr. Isabel had lost her money and tickets which were easy enough to replace, but a much deeper concern was the loss of her ID cards, including her Green card. Nevertheless, the Sisters went through the day as if nothing had happened. I wish I could say the same for myself. I was caught up in an emotional storm of hurt, anger and embarrassment. Soon enough, the sisters were off to LAX with the promise that they would let me know about their decision to come to St. Raphael.

The call came two weeks later to notify me that they had to wait six months for the decision of their Provincial Chapter. Six months came and the God who draws straight with crooked lines was active on the canvas with another surprise. Sr. Isabel was re-elected to the Provincial administration but her traveling companion, Sr. Brigida was assigned to St. Raphael.

Sr. Brigida was joined by a delightful companion, Sr. Matilde, who got a job as a chaplain at the county hospital.

Sr. Brigida was a no-nonsense leader who performed wonders during her years at the parish. She worked with families and adult sacramental preparation. She was a marvelous counselor and a companion to hundreds of troubled folk. She helped us all understand the Hispanic experience and yet was up-to-date with her theology.

A little footnote to this story is fascinating. Some five years later, Sr. Isabel was assigned to Stockholm, Sweden, where there are a large group of Mexican immigrants adding more than a little color to Sweden.

The Ministry of Goodbye

As things developed on several fronts in the parish, people began to feel both welcomed and involved. Many options were provided for the people to express their growing desire to make their faith more concrete. These activities included the liturgy and religious education, the prayer group, and the Christian Family Movement but also several programs that reached out to the needs of the neighborhood. Our participation in *One LA*, the metropolitan wide community organization, grew rapidly at this time.

In the midst of all this positive activity, I began to develop a new ministry, the ministry of saying goodbye to people. It seemed like each week several families would come to me with the same message. "Fr. Tracy, we really love what you are doing in the parish and the school. It is really exciting. But we have the chance to move and we need to get a better and safer situation for the kids. We are really going to miss St. Raphael."

These encounters were bittersweet for me. Most of these families were active and supportive of the school and parish. They were the beneficiaries of our training and formation programs. At the same time, I felt happy for them to get a safer situation for their children.

This exodus was more than met by a continuing influx of newcomers, the majority of whom were newly arrived immigrants. A great number of the newcomers had no papers.

Over the years this tremendous change gave me a strong visual image of the parish. The parish was like a river. It looks the same but underneath there is tremendous activity and change. Gradually it appears slowly different even on the top but at all times it keeps on moving.

Learning the Culture

One of the developments of Carmelite renewal is caught in the phrase "in the midst of the people." It is a call for us Carmelites to get close to the people, to cut away the obstacles of clericalism and its privileges. When I walk through the neighborhood, I have a deep sense of being "in the midst of the people." These walks, most often, are moments of grace. I often wonder how our parish fits into God's plan and love for all these people. It is a humbling experience to realize how many the parish is not reaching but God is more than up to the task. We call it the universality of grace. This major teaching of Vatican II points out that God is always active in a saving way in the lives of all human beings. More than anything else, the parish should be a sign of this universal love of God and point to this mystery in every way possible.

There are literally tens of thousands within our parish boundaries who call themselves Catholic and thousands more belonging to other Christian denominations. One day when Archbishop Gomez was here for Confirmation, he asked me, "How many people are in the parish?" I said, "It depends on which day of the year." He said that was a good answer because he was so much part of the Hispanic culture.

When I arrived at the parish I had a very special gift. I already had the experience of entering deeply into the African American culture. This allowed me to approach the experience of the Hispanic culture with a sense of humility and openness realizing that I would never totally understand it. At the same time it freed me to learn and serve as best I can.

No doubt the most fascinating event has been Ash Wednesday. After several services in the morning and early afternoon, we begin in earnest at 4:30 PM. At this time we fill the church in five minutes. Then we lock the doors, do the Service of the Word and distribute the ashes. We then dismiss the group through the front doors and fill the church again from the backdoors. This goes on continually past 9 PM. About 6,000 people receive ashes. On a good Sunday we have 1,500 in attendance.

After talking with many people, I have come to the conclusion that the Ash Wednesday experience is a religious experience for all. For some, it is a Christian religious experience.

The feast of Our Lady of Guadalupe is another cultural phenomenon. On December 12th we open the church at 4:30 AM. When we begin the service at 5 AM, the church is jammed full with hundreds standing out in the cold air of a December morning in Los Angeles. We have the morning prayer of the Church and some Aztec cultural dancing. Then thousands are fed sweet bread and coffee. As they leave several will come up to me and say, "It was very beautiful, Padre. I'll see you next year."

On this feast of the Virgin of Guadalupe I have tried to enter into the program and prayer that the people so passionately love but it just does not touch me the way it is in the blood of the people. However, I experience a deeply religious moment within my heart by being present to the awesome and simple faith of the people.

Another deeply entrenched cultural experience is the Quinceañera. At its most authentic level it is a celebration of the continuing gift of life in the community identified in the young girl coming to the age of puberty at 15. Often as celebrated today, it is encrusted with a growing level of consumerism that ends up being an expensive and fleeting event for families that could use the money for many constructive things.

When the priests talk about a "Q Mass," we label them from a 1 to 10 as an experience of the faith. A 1 on the scale would be the daughter of a committed and mature Catholic family. It is truly a spiritual experience. The 10 on the scale would be a gathering where most have no sense of what the Mass is. This would be exemplified by the following occurrence. At the practice the night before, I asked the girl if she was going to receive Communion. She asked her mother, "What is that?" A few minutes later, I asked her if she was going to bring flowers to the Blessed Virgin. Again she asked her mother, "Who is that?"

Families ranking as 8, 9, and 10 on the "Q Mass" scale are examples of how the transplanted cultural practices carry on even as they get more and more disconnected from their roots in the faith that was so richly supported by the culture in the native country. This disconnection of the culture and the faith is a growing problem in all of Hispanic life here in the US.

Other expressions of people clinging to their faith with little context is the role of holy water, images, flowers, scapulars and candles. Many people only come to the church to get holy water or candles or to have their sacred images blessed.

I often wish I had attended at the parish staff meeting of the early friars when they decided that blessing persons and things would be a good pastoral strategy. This has to have been one of the most influential decisions in the history of the Church in the Americas. Blessings are in the DNA of the Hispanic people in a profound and beautiful way.

I gradually learned to have an appreciation of these expressions of the Hispanic culture. I was also able to point out with some clarity the reality that all of these sacramentals were slowly being difused as they are removed from the support of the more deeply religious culture of the native countries.

In the midst of these expressions of popular religiosity, I presented a plan of evangelization that the parish staff helped clarify and nuance. I pictured the parish in the form of four circles with the center point being Jesus Christ in the Eucharist. We are all heading to the center by walking with Jesus.

The people in the outer circle, the fourth, are those who center their religious experience on the sacramentals. They may or may not come for Ash Wednesday but have little other contact with the parish. A funeral may be a possibility. They definitely want holy water, candles, and images.

The people in circle three seldom come to Mass but they will celebrate a Quinceañera and most will have their children baptized. They definitely will want a Christian burial.

The people in the second circle are those who come to Mass several times a year. They will make sure that their children receive First Communion and some will have their teens in the Confirmation program. Eventually, they will at least consider the possibility of having their marriage blessed by the Church. For many reasons, the marriage blessed in the Church shows a level of commitment that often leads the first circle.

Finally, those in the first circle are devoted to their faith, come to Mass regularly, and usually have some involvement in parish activities. These parishioners have several levels of involvement. They are seeking to deepen their faith by adult formation in many different ways.

The basic plan of evangelization is first and foremost to respect where people are. We try to engage them in the things that are of interest to them and always gently call them forth to the next circle, the next stage of involvement, the next stage of growth. This may vary from simply being hospitable to them when they come for holy water to introducing the Lay Carmelites to Christian meditation as an introduction to contemplative prayer. All the activities of the parish aim at moving people out of their comfort zone to the next step on the road walking with Jesus.

14

The School: the Early Days

First Impression

When I arrived I brought strong passion and high hopes for the parish school. I had learned a lot in my days in Chicago. I looked forward to great things for the school.

The reality of the school slowly frustrated my hopes and dreams. There were several things that slowly introduced me to the chaos of the school.

The first was a trampoline in the gym. I saw some kids jumping and flipping on it. They were going high and there was neither safety net nor adult supervision. It took my breath away. One small misstep and one of these kids could be a paraplegic. The trampoline was closed down and off the campus immediately.

The secretary in the school had been here for many years. As the Hispanic families gained confidence in me, I learned horror stories of her mistreatment of them. The organization of the office needed a massive upgrade.

The shock treatment continued when I was in the second grade class and learned that they were using the same work books from previous years by simply erasing the answers. To say the least, these circumstances gave a horrific first impression.

Why?

As I dug into the reasons why the school ended up in such a dire condition, it became clear that the pastors had neglected it for the past eight years. Also there were many mixed reviews of the principal. She stirred up strong feelings pro and con.

The school was woefully underfunded. In the past, the parish was a source of funds but now the parish was facing its own economic crisis. The local fundraising was minimal and sporadic and no effort was made to raise funds from outside. Also, the collection of tuition was inconsistent. The net result brought the school to the brink of disaster with no one willing to face that reality.

The principal, Mrs. Helen Martinez, had been drafted into this deteriorating situation from her job as the sixth grade teacher. She was not ready for the job but she was a worker and a survivor.

In my conversation with her she deflected all blame from herself. There was some truth in what she said. After the first year I gave her another chance with some additional resources I was beginning to bring to the school.

My response to the situation after the initial shock and terrible disappointment was to plunge in full time. I clearly had a goal. It was to change the culture of the school. I insisted that the uniform be worn and that the boys wear ties every day. I set up a program of fundraising where parents had to participate. I insisted that tuition be paid on time or the children were sent home. I set up as much support as I could for the teachers as we implemented a fair and balanced discipline program. This meant we had to remove several troubled children from the school for either the lack of support from the family or our inability to meet the special needs of the child.

I made a major upgrade in the religion program for the children. We have two grades attend Mass each Wednesday and the entire school comes to Mass on the First Friday. We made these lively and interesting liturgies with maximum participation.

I also developed a program for the acolytes. I made it "cool" to be an acolyte. At one time I had as many as ninety kids in the program but in time this number dropped to about fifty. This was much more realistic group. I became able to have a special presence in the school in this way.

Also at this time I made a connection with Dr. Robert Ibsen. He was a graduate of Mt. Carmel High School. He was founder and owner of Rembrandt toothpaste. Over the years, he became a very generous benefactor. We started out by receiving tubes of Rembrandt that were imperfect. Soon we were selling them in place of chocolate for our fundraisers. We also raised money for the parish by the sale of the toothpaste.

At this time I also started to contact some suburban schools. We were able to get books that upgraded our texts. These schools were also a source for desks, tables, and chairs.

One very positive program was the music program. We shared a music teacher with two other schools and he developed a excellent Gospel choir. His name was Peter Scott. Eventually he would help transform St. Raphael School.

As the school changed people had to face a new call to accountability. By October of the second year it was obvious that the principal, in spite of her determination and survivor skills, was not the person to carry us into the future. Helen left to work in another Catholic school before she got her doctorate. She is now doing a fine job in the public schools.

In the fall of 1995 she read the tea leaves and responded negatively. She organized a group of parents to start a petition drive to have me removed. That got my old community organizing juices flowing. Soon there was no petition drive. However, the negative atmosphere contributed nothing to the learning atmosphere in the school.

Anne Bouvet: A Major Transition

Our committee came up with a marvelous new principal, Mrs. Anne Bouvet. She was an experienced teacher in Catholic schools, a dedicated Catholic, and a first time principal with a set of skills very appropriate to our challenging situation. Anne was hard working. She was upbeat and consistent in her treatment of faculty, staff, parents, and students. She was Hispanic but open to the African American population.

Typical of her positive attitude was the way she handled a problem that came in the first letter she opened in the first day on the job. It was a bill for $20,000 from last year's fundraiser. No one knew it was outstanding. Anne said we just would work it out someway and moved on to the next issue. This was done without fanfare.

Anne increased the enrollment to capacity for the first time in decades. She handled the accreditation process and gained the full six years, the most possible which was a small miracle in itself considering the years of neglect the school had endured. Likewise, we began a long journey to update the computer technology in the school.

Anne stayed on the job for four years until travel from her home in Alhambra was just too much for her family life. When she left the progress of the school was very significant and ready for the incredible breakthroughs that were to come.

In her first month on the job the eighth grade teacher suddenly had to leave. I told Anne this is a great opportunity to hire Peter Scott in a way that would be understood by the two other schools where he was a part time music teacher and deeply loved. She said we would not be able to afford him. I told her to let me worry about the money. We got Peter and it was one of the best decisions that I was to make in my time at St. Raphael. Today he is assistant principal, teacher, basketball and football coach, music teacher, counselor, and a great presence in the school and community. His ministry has touched the lives of thousands of youngsters over the years.

The Real Saturday Night Live

One week we had a series of break-ins in the school that were very strange. All that was missing were some inconsequential things like paper, crayons, and pencils. On the other hand it frightened and upset the children and the teachers who thought about what might be next.

One young police officer was very aggravated that the school which was such a positive force in the neighborhood was the victim of this goofiness. He volunteered to come on his free time to be a security guard. It finally reached eight break-ins in less than two weeks. We set up a simple strategy. We were going to put on the lights in the entire building and one parent volunteered her watchdog to stay over for the night.

On Saturday night, I forgot to go over to the school early to turn on the lights. I went at about 7 PM and it was dark already. As I entered the hallway through the first grade classroom, the thief was standing about eight feet away with a three foot lead bar in his hand. As soon as I opened the door he said, "I'm busted. You got me." I read the scene quite differently. Here I was with my two replaced knees and he is about 30 years younger with a lead bar. I knew I was the one that was not going to get busted. I reverted to my South Side street language and gave a series of epithets and told how much grief he had given all the children and I told him to get out. All during my blundering monologue, I was slowly retreating to the exit. He said he was sorry and left by the door on the other side.

About fifteen minutes later the parent came with the watchdog and I went home to go to bed.

At midnight, I heard my doorbell. The second grade teacher was at the door saying someone was in the office. We called and the police came immediately. They were ready to go in with four men when I told them about the dog. This put the brakes on everything. They said the dog had to go. It took a half hour for the parent to come and retrieve the dog.

In the meanwhile the thief had exited through the gym with three phones from the office. I returned to bed at 1:30 AM.

At 3 AM the doorbell rang again. The police were at the door. The thief was out in the squad car and they returned the phones and asked me to identify the man. I did and went to bed again.

About a month later I went to the court hearing. The thief pled guilty even though the judge read him a long list of his rights. The judge said he would sentence him in two weeks. The thief pleaded with the judge to sentence him now because he wanted to go back to prison where he felt more at home.

I guess he figured robbing a Catholic school was the best way to get "back home."

Marco and Mark

Somehow we got funds to bring Marco Pardo on staff as a counselor. He was spectacular at the job. He set up a program to provide positive interventions where needed and prevention services to both parents and faculty. In-service training for the faculty and parenting sessions were also part of the agenda. Besides, several intern students were brought on board.

Marco then recruited his close friend, Mark Mitchell. They wrote up the first foundation grant we got for any program. Their program was called *The Good Shepherds*. This counseling program has evolved into several different forms but has been in operation for fifteen consecutive years since Marco first started it.

Mark and Marco also initiated the search for outside funds in a more organized way. After several false starts, we made a commitment to start a Development Board. I went to a workshop run by the Catholic Schools Office. The thing I remember most was that we had to ask the prospective board member to "give or get" $10,000 a year to be on the board. My, but this was a long way from my bingo days!

I was a bundle of nerves for the first two or three contacts. Eventually, I eased into a new role and really sold the very powerful message of our work St. Raphael. At the first meeting, we had twenty-five prospects. Soon we were down to twelve members and the St. Raphael Development Board was off and running. Mr. Kevin Burke, CEO of Trinity Capital, was there for the first meeting and is the driving force for the Board today.

A New Gym and an Old Coach

Mike Trueblood had been a supporter from my first month on the job. He has been especially helpful with the newsletter. He introduced me to Sharon Benoit, a publicist, who was always on the lookout to help St. Raphael. She came up with a project for our gym which was in horrible condition.

A small sports radio station was looking for a Christmas project. Sharon put a package together for them. Dr. Ibsen contributed $5,000 in advertising. The radio station plugged the companies that worked on our gym. We got a

$50,000 facelift from several different construction firms.

Now, if Hollywood were telling the story, here is how it would go. The owner of the radio station and sports network is Terry Brennan, the former coach of Notre Dame. He hears about one of his former players, the starting quarterback on his last City Champs at Mt. Carmel High School in Chicago right before he left to take over at Notre Dame. The old quarterback is now pastor in a struggling parish in South Central Los Angeles. Brennan lends a hand to the kids and fixes the gym. That's the Hollywood version and most of it is true.

15

The Middle Years at St. Raphael

Health Problems

I was hit with several minor and one major health problem in these years. In my last year at Whitefriars on December 1, 1993, I had my left knee replaced. Then in 1997 and 1998 I had two surgeries on my foot. In 2000, I had two stints put in a heart valve. In 2002, I had radical prostate surgery because of cancer. For fifteen months I wore diapers and then had a pump placed inside only to have it put in backwards. This mistake meant another surgical procedure. Two years later, in 2005, I had hernia surgery. Then I got really sick. In 2007, on vacation in Chicago, I neglected my diet and had a severe attack of diverticulitis. I lost a tremendous amount of blood. I called my regular doctor from Chicago. He told me to go to bed and have only soup. After four days I returned to Los Angeles on a Friday and had a blood test. Saturday, when they got the results, the doctor called me and told me to drop everything and go immediately to the emergency room. My blood was dangerously low and the threat of a stroke or worst was a real possibility. I was hospitalized for five days and given a program that has solved my problems in this area.

By the way, I forgot to mention I had a second knee replacement in 2001.

Right now my health is fine and people regularly say I look great.

Hanging in There

From the death of Juan Izabal in January of 1996 to the arrival of Tom Alkire, the present associate pastor, in September of 2005, there were nine and a half years. During four of those years I was the only priest in the parish.

When I had help, it was very good. Felix Rivera was here for a little more than a year. He had to return to Puerto Rico because of a family crisis. Vicente Lopez was here for six and a half years. He was a great teacher of things Hispanic, a great companion, and a fine parish priest. He was involved in many archdiocesan programs and was the *de facto* leader of the Hispanic priest group.

When Felix left, a classmate and good friend, Leo McCarthy, was provincial. Leo and I were elected to the provincial council in 1978 and served six years together. Leo never quite got my justice and peace message but he had great respect for me and my work. Nevertheless, we did have our differences.

When he was elected provincial, he gutted the justice and peace commission by naming people who knew little or had no interest in justice and peace. I went out of my way to confront him on this move. There were some improvements in this area on the next commission.

But Leo tried again. As a province, we were going to have to close some parishes because of the continuing diminishment of our numbers. Leo saw St. Raphael as an opportunity. He told me I could go back to Chicago and this would be a perfect time for the Carmelites to leave St. Raphael. I said that I would prefer to stay and prepare the people for the possibility of not having a priest. Leo reluctantly let me do this.

The Cardinal's Letter on Liturgy

In 1998, Cardinal Mahoney issued a far reaching and very progressive letter on liturgy. It fit in with all the renewal we had been working on and gave us greater incentive to continue and expand. A central point of the letter was the importance of the assembly. This connected with our parish in a strong way. One of the changes recommended that the people stand during the Eucharistic prayer. We worked hard explaining and fighting the resistance on this change. We were into it for some years until Rome squashed it and several other elements of the Cardinal's plan. The changes initiated by Mahony stressed the communal aspect of the liturgy. The changes from the Vatican stressed the importance of the cleric.

Sexual Abuse Crisis

The sexual abuse crisis, ignited by the Boston situation in 2002, hit like an earthquake in Los Angeles. It brought on months of severe depression among many priests. We had numerous special meetings in our deanery, a group of seventeen local parishes that meet regularly. Many priests were embarrassed to wear their clerical garb in public. Most were terrified of touching children.

I was very vocal in our meetings. I said the crisis was an invitation to return to the Gospel with new vigor and passion. I suggested, among other things, that we meet regularly to share the Gospel of the coming Sunday. This program was popular for while then slowly faded except for a small group. This group still meets weekly every Monday at 6:30 AM for an hour.

In the early months of the sexual abuse crisis, there were several public actions and statements about the financial troubles of the Church. In Los Angeles, Cardinal Mahony said he would not send out Christmas cards, cut ethnic ministry offices and made deep cuts to prison and campus ministry. This followed the dedication of the new $189,000,000 Cathedral. At the same time, Cardinal Law was talking about the possibility of bankruptcy in Boston.

In my little voice in the wilderness, I wrote to the parish and our benefactors that the Church is not poor. It is rich.

What the Church needs to do in this time of crisis is to rediscover its real treasure. No matter what road is taken to move out of this epochal malaise that is the U.S. Catholic Church in 2002, one component must be put front and center. The treasure is the poor in our midst. They are the road we need to travel to encounter the Gospel once again in the depth of our crisis. We need to tell the story of how our Church is serving the poor in its parishes and schools, in the shelters and clinics, in the immigration services and counseling programs, in the support for workers, and all the efforts to respect life especially the fight against abortion. We need to get the Catholic story out. We are doing the Gospel work. We need to escalate our efforts.

People are looking for a community of faith and service. They are looking for a faithful response to the pain and hopelessness, the consolation in trial and the celebration of life. We, as Church, need to refocus ourselves as a people of the Gospel. The encounter with the poor is a key ingredient in this journey.

A few generations back a great many of our parishes and schools and hospitals and universities were built with the nickels and dimes of a poor immigrant people, most likely your parents or grandparents. This is what people saw in the Church – an invitation to life and to hope. We need to see the same today. We need to rediscover the human face of our treasure.

I do not want to be simplistic. We are in a crisis of great magnitude that will not go away easily or quickly. There needs to be a just response to the horror and a call for accountability at all levels. Yet, I need to say forcefully, one simple component of any solution will be our making central to our self-understanding as a community of faith, the service of the poor. This is the stuff of the Gospel.

Two Special Priests

Over the years the deanery in our area has had an exceptional quality of priests. We work on many common projects such as immigration and offer support and good pastoral ideas to one another.

There are two diocesan priests that have been an enormous inspiration and help to me in many ways. Tim Dyer was the pastor of the two parishes to the north of me and Dave O'Connell, a truly humorous Irishman, is the pastor to the south of me. Both are exceptional pastors, leaders and the source of many creative pastoral initiatives for me. For over ten years we have shared the Scriptures weekly and carried the cross with one another through many a dark valley. In the end we have survived and prospered, in good part, because of our mutual support and commitment.

The Phone Call

At this time of darkness and despair in the Church, I had one of those peek-a-boo moments where God shows his presence briefly but in awesome beauty. I was celebrating a First Friday school mass for the entire school. I was in the middle of my homily and my cell phone started to ring. I proved to be still quick on my feet and I answered the call. I had a little conversation and hung up. I told the kids, "that was Jesus calling and he told me to tell you he loves you all very dearly and he hopes you will all continue to do your school work and help your families." Depending on the age, the children responded with awe or a good laugh at how Fr. Tracy handled the situation.

A few months later one of the first graders came to me with a look of deep concern on his face. He asked, "Fr. Tracy, can you do me a favor. I have a problem and I need Jesus' phone number to ask for some help."

Letter from the Pastor

In the spring of 2002, I wrote the following letter in the Sunday bulletin. It captures in a special way what we had been working on in the parish as we gathered the people, told the story, and broke the bread.

"During this time, life goes on at St. Raphael. We have several people dying of cancer. Others are caught up in the slow, agonizing aging process. We are preparing First Communion for 150 children and confirmation for 50 young people. We have youngsters starting the slow, painful death of drugs. Others are using their newly discovered sexuality in destructive ways. We have parents continuing to grow in love and service of one another and their children. We have people struggling to get better jobs and better housing. We have loads of kids blowing the opportunity to get a good education while surrendering to the call of the streets. We have some of our graduates going to the finest universities and many, many more making a great sacrifice getting into a junior college. Many new babies continue to come to Mass for the first time each week. Many other children abandon the practice of Sunday Mass. Some are struggling with the magnificent process of recovery from their addiction while a few others see the life of "the seller" as a great deal that can solve their money woes in a hurry.

And the beat goes on!

In the midst of it all, this continuous flow of sin and grace, the weeds and the wheat, that is the stuff of our daily lives, we have the unending call of Jesus, the Crucified and Risen Savior, who is our Good Shepherd. He calls us all to walk with him and to choose life not death. Both life and death are happening around us every day. Let us proclaim with our lives there is reason for hope and there is new life when we walk with Jesus. There is a message of joy: Our God is a God of love who will overcome all the expressions of death if we let Him become our Good Shepherd.

And the beat goes on!

But not without hope and not without a faith community that is open to the wonder of a loving God whose call to new life is always present whether it be in the midst of the darkest moments or the wonder of falling in love."

16

The School: Time of Transformation

The Arrival of the Barbara "Whirlwind"

Early on in my time in Los Angeles, I became involved in the schools. The archdiocese had a committee of pastors as an advisory group called PACE, the Pastors' Committee on Education. I became a member in my first year and was chairmen for several years until it was dissolved. In this position I became well known at the schools' office.

When I heard that Anne Bovet was leaving, I cashed in all my chips to get information on the best possible candidates to replace her. I had one ready to sign a contract as our committee accepted one final interview in May 2000.

After the interview with a recent graduate of a new master in arts program at Loyola Marymount University for Catholic school principals, the committee was gushing with excitement. They asked how I felt. I said that I was upset and angry because now I had to bring bad news to a gentleman I assured of the job. There was no question we had to take Barbara Curtis. We have been the benefactors of a great school ever since.

Barbara brought an exceptional set of educational skills to carry the school to new level of excellence. She also brought a combination of intelligence and enthusiasm that produced incredible results in her normal 60 plus hour week. What surprised me the most, however, was her ability to handle the wide range of parental emotions that go with the intensity of living in the pressure cooker that is South Central. This can be challenging for any administrator.

Added to the above was Barbara's past life as a suburban mother who was experienced in fundraising for an elite private Catholic elementary school and as an active parent at Loyola High. Those skills helped her to more than double our budget during her first ten years as principal. Two programs initiated by Cardinal Mahony were crucial to Barbara's struggle to meet the financial challenge.

All the inner city Catholic schools and parishes had the helpful support of these exceptional programs. The first was *Together in Mission*. Each parish was taxed 10 percent of the previous years' Sunday collection. This was distributed to the poorest parishes and schools. It was essential for our survival. The second program was the *Catholic Education Foundation*. This program distributed several thousand scholarship grants to needy families. It has been integral to our survival and helped us serve the truly needy.

Our venture into a Development Board was just off the ground when Barbara arrived. She was critical to its growth and progress.

Barbara built upon the order that Anne Bouvet had brought to the academic program. However, her gift was to get resources and personnel in an unprecedented manner. Soon, we had computers in every classroom, then we a computer lab, then we the entire school wired for the internet, then we had extensive training workshops for the teachers, then we had a laptop for each student in fourth grade, then we had smart boards in every grade and then we had more workshops for teachers and the beat goes on. The technology revolution is impossible to keep up with but at times, it seems, Barbara has lapped the field.

Fr. Al Koppes is a Carmelite who has survived and even prospered among the Jesuits at Loyola Marymount University for over forty years. One of his many contributions was a program called PLACE. In this program new college grads spend two years teaching in an inner city Catholic school. At the same time they earn a master's and teaching certificate. Barbara has been deeply involved in helping young teachers come to St. Raphael School through this program. We have had at least one of these young teachers on our faculty each and every year of the program.

The Bush educational program, *No Student Left Behind*, has contributed to the financial burden on our school since almost our entire faculty has taken advantage of this program to get an master's degree. This, of course, meant a substantial blessing for our students but it also meant a well earned salary increase for the teachers.

Barbara used the talents of Mr. Peter Scott to develop a fine music program and a great Gospel choir. Likewise, there was an explosion in the athletic program. There are teams for boys and girls in basketball and volleyball at two levels and a girls' softball team and a boys' soccer team. Mr. Scott handles the upper grade basketball for both boys and girls. The boys have made it to the final four in a field of 150 CYO teams in four of the last seven years. Peter also created a culture of excellence for a school theatrical presentation that attracts huge crowds every December. They are exceptional performances with contributions from each grade.

All of this, and the counseling program, have been made possible by Barbara's ability to garner outside resources. One of the best moves was a oundation grant to hire a person to work in the area of development. We ired Elizabeth Agustin who is a talented writer of grants. We have played he foundation game with considerable skill when Barbara and Elizabeth join heir talents in this area.

Barbara had a dream to have a Pre-K program. She mentioned it to someone at the Catholic Schools office. John and Dorothy Shea, extraordinary philanthropists for the archdiocese, had a deep desire to help the Catholic schools and the money to do it. We were the first on a long list of incredible gifts they have distributed.

When I heard they were coming to our campus. I assumed they were on a tour of various schools to get the lay of the land and make a decision about where to give their money. I was wrong. They made a commitment to a new Pre-Kindergarten on the first visit.

Then things slowed down as the search for the owner of the apartment building next to the school, the planned site of the new Pre-Kindergarten, was hidden under a layer of deception. I then made an alternative proposal. I suggested that they tear down our old convent and build a new building using the money they were to pay for the land of the apartment building and give us a meeting room, offices for religious education, and a kindergarten. These were the activities we housed in the old convent. They agreed and in 2004 we dedicated a new Mt. Carmel Center of 8,700 square feet at the cost of $1.4 million. It was as if it dropped straight down from heaven. The upgrade of our programs from the old convent was remarkable.

While all this was going on, two forces were pulling in opposite directions for Catholic schools. The growth of charter schools was one transforming factor in the education scene in Los Angeles. They were expanding rapidly and affecting the Catholic school population especially among African Americans.

The second issue was the growing awareness that the Catholic parish school has to be part of the evangelization program of the parish. As a result of these two forces, Barbara and I made two foundational moves that had consequences for all the inner city Catholic schools.

The Catholic Educational Foundation, which granted millions of dollars in scholarship grants annually, realized that a crisis was coming for the Catholic schools, especially in the inner city. They knew part of it was that many pastors and, in particular, the growing number of pastors who were foreign born, did not understand their role as pastor in the school.

I was asked to give the keynote speech at a gathering of pastors in early fall of 2008. My message was clear and powerful. The school is a very important part of the evangelization mission of the parish. We need to make the schools instruments of evangelization. We need to destroy the frequently destructive division, and often times, isolation of the school from the parish.

At the same time, Barbara heard of a program out of Cincinnati that was having great success in marketing Catholic schools. She gathered four other principals to get enough funding to bring the leader of this program to Los Angeles. This, in turn, has led to the development of a well-organized marketing program that has been helpful to the schools. Our school has received many benefits from this effort including a grant to develop a top-notch web site.

Like everybody else, we were rocked by the economic downfall of 2009. Barbara had positioned us to survive because of her many initiatives, especially the marketing.

Just recently, we were gifted with the call to join the efforts of the Specialty Foundation. In this program, twenty-four inner city Catholic schools are given a fully paid professional to raise funds and resources for the school. Ms. Elva Lopez joined us in early 2013.

A Child in Every Desk

Another interesting development came from a project of our Regional Bishop, Edward Clark. He convened a committee of four pastors, four principals, the superintendent, and a school supervisor. I was one of the pastors. The committee hoped to face the crisis by asking how we can save our Catholic schools. Over several sessions, there was a change of focus. It moved from saving the schools to filing every desk in the schools. The goal of having Catholic schools create leaders for both the Church and society proved to be a creative paradigm shift with important consequences for our pastoral planning for the schools.

> "Our concern is not saving our schools. Our real concern is providing a Catholic education for as many Catholic students as possible. Our goal is to fill every available desk with a student who will be a credit to Catholic education, a student who is well-formed in the faith and who will use his or her influence constructively in the world. If we can do that, we will never have to focus simply on saving our schools." (Bishop Clark)

For many decades Catholic schools have worked to create leaders for society. The idea of creating leaders for the Church has been in a slow but steady decline. Earlier in the year I asked my faculty if they had ever asked or encouraged any of their students to consider becoming a nun or a priest. The answer was that not one of the teachers had.

A constant complaint of pastors has been that the families in the school do not participate in the Sunday Eucharist or the life of the parish. The document of the educational summit calls for a different approach. If the governing principle is to educate and form future Catholic leaders for the Church and for society, then very often we are educating the wrong children if their families are far removed from consistent practice of the faith. Leaders for the future Church will only come from families of faith.

While not neglecting the basic evangelical task to encourage all school families to participate in the full life of the parish, the document encourages pastors to recruit the active members of the parish to place their children in the school.

In 2012 I established a group to model this goal of creating leaders for the Church. I call them "The Carmelites." They are twelve upper grade students who are chosen on the basis of two criteria: they are good and faithful acolytes and they come from families that are active participants in the faith life of the parish.

During the summer I had several sessions with these students to prepare them for a special role in the liturgy for the school masses. They are trained as sacristans, commentators, ushers and leaders to help the classes in the responses at the Masses. Their next task will be to prepare the children who read and do the petitions at liturgy.

In our weekly meeting the youngsters continue to learn more about the liturgy. Along with an introduction to the Carmelites as a religious order and our vision and history, we have begun the practice of *lectio divina*.

Another area in which they are leaders is the environmental program in the school. This includes helping with the recycling of various lunchtime items. In September they participated in an environment day under the sponsorship of a local group, *Heal the Bay*. They had more than fifty families go out into the neighborhood to pick up trash that otherwise would end up killing the marine life in the ocean.

The group of leaders was invested at the Sunday liturgy and at a school assembly. They received a brown shirt with the word *Carmelites* and the shield of the Order on it. They wear the shirt any time they function as leaders in the school liturgies or in one of their service projects.

I asked them why they felt it was important to be a member of "The Carmelites." Guadalupe Serrano responded "because I get to teach other people to learn about the Church and get closer to God." Ricky Guevara replied, "You can help people in need in our community" and "walk with Jesus."

One morning four fourth graders ran up to me on the playground and asked excitedly and all together, "When can we become Carmelites?" Then I knew, my new program was on target.

The vision contained in Bishop Clark's document brings together the three activities of Barbara in marketing, Elva in fund raising and mine in evangelizing to give us a clear picture of what we have to do: recruit from the active parish families. These, for the most part, are poor Hispanic families who would never have thought of the possibility of their children going to a Catholic school because in their country Catholic schools are for the rich.

As we set out on this program, we came to where we had started 130 years ago with Catholic schools: a program to give the poor immigrants an opportunity to make it in society and to develop and enhance their faith. So too, I have come full circle from the parish school that was replaced by the *Chicago Plan* and then the "Servant School." If we are successful, we will have a school that is poorer and more Catholic.

Now that we got that straight, all we need to do is raise the money for the tuition. At the same time we will give an education where up to 95 percent of our graduates will enter college which is the most functional program in our society to end poverty.

I Want to Walk with Jesus

In my first two years after arriving in Los Angeles, and to a lesser degree with Anne Bouvet, I was involved in the administration of the school. With the arrival of Barbara Curtis, I felt no need in this area. I do continue to work with development and the religion program.

We have always had a weekly Wednesday Mass for two grades. Then, on first Friday, we have a Mass for the entire school. I have a gift to be able to preach in a dynamic way to all the grades and all the grades together at these masses. They are almost always good experiences for the children. Of course, there are exceptions. One of these was the first time the kindergarten class was at the mass. I went to their room after the mass to see how they did. Most had a good time. However, Paul was quite truthful and said, "Man, I thought I would never get out of there!" I could identify with Paul from my incredibly long afternoons of hardly surviving the Stations of the Cross at St. Laurence.

Over time I have created a theme that gives a context to the particular reflections of the homily. I constantly have the children repeat in all kinds of groupings and in different voices, "I want to walk with Jesus." Over the years, this simple mantra has sunk in. I knew, again, that I had gotten the message across when a little first grader came to me on the playground and said, "When are we going to have Mass again? I want to walk with Jesus."

17

The Parish: A Time of Maturing

A Really Bad Three Months

I remember reading an old Jewish maxim that says "God is not a kindly old uncle but a tornado." Well the tornado hit us in full force in the early months of 2003. Death and injury from drive-by shootings, sexual abuse and rape, violence in the families caused by drugs and alcohol, the death of a single parent with an only child, and other manifestations of aggression and hostility succeeded each other in rapid fashion in our parish and school community. It seemed as if we received the condensed version of three years of troubles in three months.

The Easter message of that year about life coming out of death was so apparent in the loving response of so many people to these tragedies. Even though these horror stories are the daily stuff of the headlines, it is very different when it strikes you at home. Yet the profound experience of love and compassion did unveil this God of the tornado who draws life out of the destructive violence. It is in times like these that the special gift of our Catholic faith as a sacramental Church shines forth. Not only do we have the sacraments as an outward sign of God's presence, we also have the sign of the community as a sacrament of God's presence when we are faithful to the call to serve and love one another and to walk together holding hands. Once again, we learned the lesson that we are called to give hope to each other. We are called to be the face and hands of a God who has not forsaken us in the darkness of violence and destruction.

During this time at St. Raphael we discovered the gift of giving hope and comfort to one another. We became the sacrament of a God who hears the cry of the poor by simply being present to one another in the emergency rooms, the police station, at the funeral parlors, and just sitting around the table breaking bread. Several mothers, in particular, were beacons of light in the quiet strength in the midst of their tragic family pain.

You know, this is an old story. But it becomes new with each tornado. We consistently learn that the grace is in the struggle. What we learn is that the struggle will not end but will continue to invite us to be the sacrament of God's presence to one another. Some years ago I ran across this quote from Thomas Merton, the Trappist monk and writer who many consider one of the great Christians of the 20th Century. It has been a guiding light for me over the years and was especially fitting in the context of our tornadoes at that time.

> "All the good you will do will not come from you but from the fact that you have allowed yourself, in obedience of faith, to be used by God's love. Think of this more and gradually you will be free from the need to prove yourself, and you will be more open to the power that will work through you from the need to prove yourself, and you will be more open to the power that will work through you without you knowing it. If you can get free of the domination of causes and first serve Christ's truth, you will be able to do more and be less crushed by the inevitable disappointments. The real hope, then, is not in something we think we can do, but in God who is making something good out of it in some way we cannot see. If we can do His will, we will be helping in the process. But, we will not necessarily know about it beforehand." [14]

When we celebrated Easter in 2003, we knew in a special way that our hope was restored to continue the struggle. The streets had not won the battle. We continued to celebrate life in our children and one another.

A New Problem Fixer

Esther Manriquez was in her early eighties and fighting a good fight to stay on the job.She reluctantly surrendered the hard fight in stages. Her first move was to move from the parish office to the religious education office. Then she decided to go half a day. Finally, one day, she just said it was enough. The very next day she entered a nursing home where she remains happily as the superstar of trivia games among her many other accomplishments.

Esther's replacement was Ms. Ena Duran. She is the single mother of four daughters and a gifted person of faith. She has effectively grown into the role of parish manager and brings a sensitive and compassionate touch to all levels of administration.

She presently is in her third year of studies at Mount St. Mary's weekend college for adults. The parish is the beneficiary at many levels of her expanding horizons as she moves toward her baccalaureate degree.

Ena has a good grasp of the total operation of the parish. She anticipates problems before they happen and moves toward a quick and fair resolution when they do happen. This talent is most often a hidden but invaluable contribution to the well-being of the faith community at St. Raphael.

Mariachi

Jaime Morales left the staff after four years to become a social worker. However, he quickly returned in 1998 as a volunteer extraordinaire. He developed a program to train children in music and instruments to form a mariachi group. This involved two hours of practice after school for three nights a week. Most children learned the violin and guitar but a few learned the trumpet or the base.

The group soon started playing at the 8 AM Mass and now has been doing so for over fifteen years. They began playing at social events that helped pay for their uniforms and other goodies for the children. Jaime served twelve years as director. When he left, I was sure this program would fade away. It has not and continues to flourish with a new teacher and the strong involvement of the new parents.

The program has helped over five hundred youngsters learn how to play an instrument. It also is a great teacher of Mexican culture. One other strong benefit has been the academic growth of the youngsters. The discipline of regular practice, the performance schedule and the growth in the knowledge of music have provided a great foundation for academic performance.

The core members of the first group hung in for several years while continually adding new members. Some of the youths last just a short time but the average is over three and a half years. This provides a strong continuity. There are always novices beginning the journey.

The first graduates of the program set a pattern of high standards. They all ended up in top-notch universities. The pattern has continued in a little less spectacular but meaningful way with most going to good colleges and universities. A significant number of children have gone to higher level programs of music studies and performance. Most recently, one of our teenage girls was in a group of eight special students who traveled and performed in a one week trip to London with the Los Angeles Philharmonic Orchestra.

Prayer Garden

When the Shea family came to visit and commit to a new building, one of the members of their group was Brother Hilarion. He is the man in charge of the archdiocesan office for construction. Over the years he has been helpful to St. Raphael. At the end of that momentous visit, I asked Brother Hilarion to look at another small problem we had. Next to the west side of our parish office, which is in the rectory, was a chain link fence that separated a walkway from a rather ugly and grubby alley way. The week before Esther had looked out of the window and to her shock, saw a dead body there. We learned that it was a murder victim from the San Fernando Valley about thirty miles away.

I asked Brother Hilarion to help us. He did in a big way. He put up a cinderblock wall to replace the fence and give us more privacy, then sent in a crew to sand and varnish the wooden floors in the first floor of the rectory and to paint several rooms.

So with the new wall and the coming of the new building, I challenged the parish to do something creative with the new space on the side of the rectory. I invited them to leave a gift to future generations. The result was has been a beautiful prayer garden.

In this prayer garden, we have a small shrine to the favorite saint of each ethnic group in the parish, a beautiful plaza with a shrine to Our Lady of Mt. Carmel and a special and significant plaque to remember Mt. Carmel High School and hundreds of rose bushes. It is a quiet and peaceful oasis in the midst of troubled South Central Los Angeles.

The Arrival of the Belizeans

Around this time (2006-10), an increasing number of Belizeans joined the parish. These people were immigrants from Belize, the former British Honduras. They are African American and English speakers for the most part.

The Belizeans come from two main groups. They are the Creoles and the Garifuna. The latter group has a fascinating story. Although they are African American, they claim they were never in slavery. They escaped from the slave boats and ended up in the mountains where they maintained their African language and culture.

The Creoles were the beneficiaries of a great English education system and are generally more socially advanced than the Garifuna.

Another division among the Belizeans is language. Those people who live near the border of Guatemala or Mexico often speak only Spanish. Most people from of the rest of the country speak English or are bi-lingual.

Mrs. Alice Augustine has been a long time leader in the parish and in the Belizean Garifuna community. She has been influential in the positive development of the growing Belizean population in the parish. During the past few years, we have been gifted with a special choir of about twenty members. They are called "The Village Voices." All of the members come from the same village as Alice Augustine in Belize. Part of their unique and lively repertoire includes traditional Catholic hymns from the forties and fifties.

We Finally Got Together

In 2005, just in time to watch the historic White Sox World Series, Fr. Tom Alkire came to St. Raphael from his assignment of five years in Torreon, Mexico.

I met Tom Alkire in my Latin class in my first year at Mt. Carmel High School in 1950. Four years later, we left together to go to the Carmelite seminary in Niagara Falls and to join a class of forty-four other seminarians. Eventually, eight of us were ordained. Tom and I are among the survivors. When we finished the ten years of rigorous seminary training in 1964, Tom and I went in separate directions. After a few years in high school ministry, Tom went to Chile where he began a lifetime of ministry to poor Hispanics. Along the way, he developed a charismatic prayer style that influences his ministry. In 2005, Tom brought a rich history, plenty of enthusiasm, and a simple and humble lifestyle to St. Raphael. We have worked well together for our years together here in the parish.

Change in the Neighborhood

Around 2005, I began to notice a change in the neighborhood. The first hint came from the clearest indicator of the population, Ash Wednesday. I began to see two things. First, it was taking a little longer to fill the church before the services. Then, the later services did not fill the worship space. There were actually empty pews. Then I saw another new phenomenon that I had never seen in all my time at the parish. I saw "for rent" signs. Previous to this time, there almost always was a waiting list for apartments.

In this changing set of circumstances in the neighborhood, we began a campaign in 2006 to protest the construction of a new elementary school just three blocks away from an existing school. An entire block of homes and apartments was about to be demolished to make space for the new facility. In a meeting with the Councilman, Bernard Parks, I mentioned my observation of the shrinking population based on my Ash Wednesday observations. He was respectful but dubious. Two years later, government figures caught up with my Ash Wednesday numbers and showed a pattern of real change, a strong movement following the decade of overcrowding.

I began to observe two other things happening in the parish. Fewer newcomers were arriving, changing a longstanding pattern. Likewise, fewer people were leaving the parish. My image of the parish as a river was fading away. The result was a little more stability in the neighborhood and that had a lot of positive results.

The changes went into high gear with the economic crisis of 2009. The neighborhood was really different. People were locked into the neighborhood with few able to move out and up. Others were locked out because of new and stringent border enforcement. The lack of jobs reduced the attraction dramatically.

Safeguard the Children

In 2007 we were chosen as one of a handful of parishes in the Archdiocese to participate in a national audit to see how faithful and effective the parishes were in responding to the bishops' program to protect the children. The program, which came out of the historic Dallas meeting of the bishops, was very demanding and meticulous. We had done our homework and, with a little overtime work, we were able to organize our paperwork to be ready for whatever the audit wanted to know.

All of this included making sure that any person who had contact with the children in the parish or in the school had to meet the standards and requirements of the program. These consisted of the following:

1. Each person must be fingerprinted so the authorities could check for any past criminal activities;

2. Each person must attend a three hour class on sexual abuse including the proper way to respect boundaries;

3. The parish must make sure all this activity for each person was documented and on an accessible public file;

4. The parish must have a program of ongoing education on the topic of sexual abuse;

5. The school must provide training for teachers and catechists to teach the children about boundaries;

6. The parish and school must identify those who are responsible to report sexual abuse and all the particulars of how this was to be done.

All this led me to appreciate how the Church has responded to the crisis. We surely do not get credit, and probably do not deserve credit, given the length and depth of our denial and neglect, but a great amount has been done.

Right at the time of the audit, our teachers and catechists, having received special training, began classes in "Good Touch/Bad Touch" for all the children. This "Good Touch/Bad Touch" extended the influence of the message into the home where the violation is most often a well kept secret.

The need for this expansion was urgent. The statistics are startling. One in three females and one in five males are sexually abused in the U.S. before they are eighteen years of age. The overwhelming amount of sexual abuse happens in the home in the context of the family.

Think about it. Tens of thousands of parishes across the country will reach out in a meaningful way to protect the children from this "dirty little secret" in our midst. Surely, this program will reveal traumatic circumstances in numerous households, but imagine how many children will be protected as we place the spotlight on this evil with ever greater intensity.

There are no headlines about this program being implemented in every Catholic parish. Yet, it is a powerful event that reaches into the bowels of evil and protects children from a lifetime of trauma that comes from sexual abuse. Even in the horrendous weeds of this curse, we have the wheat of a late but positive response.

18

The Parish: Continuing Growth

Who Makes Decisions?

Over the years I have had numerous pastoral councils. They were never a great success, and most often, not even a moderate success. It was always a struggle to get the members to see the large picture of the parish. What was useful was the attention given to concerns of the various groups in the parish. Mrs. Theresa Roche, a tireless worker, was an outspoken advocate for the shrinking African American community. Because of her constant presence and ability to grow, Theresa adjusted beautifully to embrace the growing complexity of the larger focus of the parish. Likewise, Alice Augustine had been a gentle but steady voice for the Belizeans. She too, over the years, grew to see the larger picture with significant depth.

Fr. Vicente knew the practical interest of the Hispanics and set up a monthly meeting of leaders of the various groups. This forum has grown over the years to be a meaningful voice of their concerns. I have never once attended their meeting as a way of empowerment. I respected their desires whenever possible and explained my reasons on the very few times I had to go against their decisions.

The parish staff consists of Barbara Curtis, principal; Maria Moran, religious education director; Ena Duran, secretary/parish manager; Harry Wiley, director of liturgy; Carolina Hernandez, coordinator of Confirmation; Fr. Tom; and me. We meet regularly every two weeks and spend the first part of the meeting reflecting and sharing the coming Sunday's Gospel. All the basic policy and necessary details of administrative and schedule items make up the content of these meetings. The basic direction of the parish is guided by this group which has plenty of input from the various groups in the parish.

As pastor I have always felt one of my most essential responsibilities is to keep communication open among all the varying, and often conflicting, interest groups in the parish. This most often was accomplished at the staff meetings.

Whole Community Catechesis

In 2003, the archdiocese invited all the parishes to a presentation on a new approach to catechesis. It stressed the need to work with all ages and groups in the catechetical program. We bought into the new approach with great enthusiasm.

The parish added two wonderful programs to implement this innovative approach. They are adult retreats and faith assemblies for the parents. The retreats are structured as a one day event to call the adults to a conversion experience. Members of the parish make the presentations and do all the organizing. The priests hear confessions and celebrate the Eucharist. We have had dozens of these retreats over the past ten years with great blessings for individuals and for our faith community as a whole.

In the faith assemblies we recruit the parents of the First Communion children. We insist that the parents attend twelve sessions of about two hours each. We can do this because these parents have such a strong desire to have their children receive First Communion. Often they do not understand the pressure of the culture that influences them in this process.

I enjoy watching the parents coming to the first session. They look like they are entering the Dachau prison camp of Nazi Germany. They are deeply conflicted. They want their kids to receive First Communion. They absolutely do not want to come to these sessions. Only a handful of about one hundred families see the need for this program. However, since we draw the line in the sand, they come.

After one or two sessions they begin to enjoy the time because it connects to their reality.

The content is a basic outline of Salvation History with an introduction to the Bible and, most especially, an encounter with Jesus Christ. The message is that they are the primary teachers of their children. They need to know the message to share the message.

We do all that with presentations that stress much discussion at tables in small groups. They see themselves in the Scriptures for the first time and it is both fascinating and life giving. The break with coffee and sweet bread is an important element of further sharing and socializing. The sessions are given in English with simultaneous translation in Spanish. The Monday night session averages around sixty parents and a repeat session on Saturday gets about forty parents.

As many as fifty percent of the parents use this time to take the next step to a more serious commitment in their faith. In terms of our evangelization circles, this means those in circle two make a serious effort to attend mass on a regular basis. Others come to a new sense of interest once in a while but they feel a new responsibility for the faith development of their children.

At the first session I tell the parents they never would have come if I just invited them. When I ask them why they want to have their children make First Communion, almost all are really at a loss to explain.

At the last class they are effusive in their gratitude and promise to be faithful but too often the spirit is willing but the soccer game is calling!

Nevertheless, this program of the faith assemblies makes a real contribution to our effort to proclaim Jesus as our Lord and Savior.

Immigration

In the spring of 2001 a buzz went through the parish and more so in the wider Hispanic community. It was about a big march to support a change in immigration policy. Each day it escalated dramatically. I was getting a feeling similar to the high points in the Civil Rights days in the sixties. I knew it was going to be a big event. I never dreamed how big.

My marching days were over, so I blessed several buses leaving the parish and went inside to watch it on TV. I remember that the police said they anticipated a crowd of 7,500. Their last estimate was 500,000 and many reliable sources said it was a million participants.

From the point of view of attendance, it was an organizer's dream. From the point of view of the message, it was on organizer's nightmare. The Mexican flags were not well received across the country. Even more importantly the sheer volume cast waves of fear and panic into the hearts of conservatives. A backlash developed overnight and remains strong to this day. In the long run, that first march was counterproductive and ultimately, disheartening, in the Hispanic community.

So when President Obama's first venture at a comprehensive immigration program was crushed decisively, he pumped up his border patrol and his program of deportation to historic levels. This created an atmosphere of unprecedented fear among those who were not blessed with legal documents to justify their residence.

Mothers went to work at factories where they lived in a consuming fear that they would not go home to see their children that night. A simple thing like driving your car became a hard decision weighing the need to support one's family and the possibility of being picked up and deported. It was a mean and frightening atmosphere.

We had a powerful experience in the parish that captured many of the heights and depths of this situation for millions of people in our midst.

Juan and Jose were people whom many would label illegal aliens. I called them parishioners. Both men were in the country for over twenty years and had families with three young children.

One day a few summers back they were approaching a red light in their cars. Juan was late for work. Jose was on the way to his lawyer. Their choices at that moment led to two life changing phone calls to their wives.

Juan ran the red light and was caught. He had no license and consequently, no insurance and an outstanding misdemeanor charge. He was handed over to the federal authorities and quickly deported.

Jose was bringing a payment to his lawyer to set up his return to Mexico. After a three month wait in his native country, away from his family, and at great emotional and financial cost, he eventually received his green card for legal residence. His call to his wife was the conclusion of a struggle of several years and almost $15,000 in fees and penalties. However, in the end, the relief was incredible. A few days after his return, he came proudly and joyfully to show me his driver's license.

The phone call to Juan's wife was indescribably tragic. The authorities in Arizona called to say he had died trying to cross the desert. They were shipping Juan's ashes to her. The funeral mass was one of the most trying moments for me and hundreds of others as we attempted simply to be with the widow and children in this horrendous tragedy. The human face of the immigration problem was all too real!

My first response was to schedule a bi-monthly Mass of solidarity with the undocumented where they could share their story and others were able to offer words of support. The undocumented were grateful for even this minimal sign of support and hope at a time of true darkness in the first years of the Obama administration.

I then went to the deanery and along with Dave O'Connell, our dean, pushed for a program of support for the many residents in our parishes who are in need of any kind of solidarity and hope. We stressed that we were able to do only two things as pastors. We were able to put a human face on the issue that had been controlled by the propaganda on the political right as solely a legal issue. We also could bring it to prayer and wait for any political development that we could move into with a meaningful and deeply rooted voice of support.

Some of the younger priests expressed a sense of hopelessness. As this feeling got stronger in the group, I shared my experience of working in the early days in support of the peace pastoral and against nuclear escalation in 1981 and 1982. My first five workshops came up completely empty, not a single person showed up. A short fourteen months later, I was leading a march of 50,000 on the issue. In fact, the turn around on the Immigration Bill after Obama's re-election is even more dramatic.

The Young People Have Arrived

Over our latter years here at St. Raphael, Fr. Tom Alkire and I had been blessed with the opportunity to share our Carmelite life and mentor several young Carmelites.

In 2005, Boniface, a Kenyan Carmelite at the Carmelite Studies program at Washington Theological Union, asked to do some ministry in the US in this once in a lifetime opportunity. He had studied his theology in Spain, so he was fluent in Spanish. Besides, Hollywood was in Los Angeles, so he wanted to come to St. Raphael.

Bonnie really loved Los Angeles and made sure he got to see all that interested him about Hollywood. It was quite an exciting time for him. He soon learned that St. Raphael was much more fascinating than the movie capital of the world. Boniface is now the superior of a growing group of Carmelites in Nairobi, Kenya.

Fabio Rojas was a Mexican student who transferred from the New York Province of Carmelites. He spent two years with us as a brother candidate. He was extremely helpful in the citizenship class. He is an artist and left us a few major works in prominent places in the parish.

Jesus Larios, a Carmelite from our program in Mexico, joined us from September 2008 to May 2009. He was in his diaconate year. It was interesting to see him connect with the Mexican immigrants in a new cultural context.

Jesus had a great year and learned a great deal about ministry. Several of us from the parish joined him for his ordination in his hometown of Colima in April 2009. He is now an associate pastor in Torreon, Mexico.

Edgar Lopez was assigned to St. Raphael in September 2008. He was an intern here and spent most of his time working in the school.

Edgar was an immigrant from Guatemala as a youth. He grew up in North Hollywood and entered the Carmelites from our parish, St. Jane Frances de Chantal, where he was ordained on May 11, 2013.

Tony Masurkiewicz brought quite a résumé when he arrived in September 2009. He is a graduate of Mt. Carmel High School in Chicago and Yale

University where he had an excellent record of scholarship and sports. He played for teams in Chicago that won four consecutive state football championships. He was captain of his Yale football team. Just to brake the pattern, he became a member of the notorious Skull and Bones Society at Yale.

The Order planned for Tony to go on for higher studies in Carmelite spiritually. He asked if he could have a break in his studies for a year to get experience working with the poor. We were delighted he chose St. Raphael for this year. Tony made a marvelous impression with the people and was given an opportunity to truly expand his horizons which were pretty broad already.

Finally, all the way from Taiwan, the parish welcomed Joseph Wu. Joseph has an unusual story. He grew up as a Buddhist in Taiwan. At the age of thirteen he migrated with his family to Ecuador. He attended high school there and worked in the family restaurant. When he was twenty-one Joseph and the family were on the move again. This time they came to Los Angeles.

Joseph had been intrigued with Catholicism which he learned about from a close friend who became a Jesuit. So shortly after his arrival in Los Angeles Joseph entered the RCIA program and became a Catholic in a Chinatown parish. Eventually, he chose the Carmelites in his discernment of a religious order vocation because our prayer emphasis connected to his Buddhist background.

Unlike the other young men who had preceded him, Joseph was assigned to St. Raphael for six years much to the delight of the parishioners who were grateful for his predecessors but wanted a more permanent relationship.

Several months after his ordination in April 2012, I developed a program of intern pastor and gave Joseph the authority to run the parish while I maintained my pastoral role in the school. He has found it challenging and engaging. I have been on an in-house sabbatical to write this book while Joseph brought his gifts to the parish. I always say that the parish is run by 90 percent of the psychic needs of the pastor. This is holding true with Joseph as he brings a Chinese business sense that I would never have in a million years.

This past Easter 2013, Joseph baptized his mother, father, and sister into the Catholic faith.

19

The Contemplative Switch

New Turf: Aging

When I arrived here at St. Raphael, I had a clear notion of staying six years and returning to Chicago. After two years here that idea had faded. I was totally invested in the life of the parish and loved the people. The thought of leaving disappeared.

In a few months I will begin my twentieth year here. This is exceptional even in these days of the priests' shortage. Having been here all this time, I have been able to enter into the lives of the people in special ways. From birthday parties to visits in the jail, helping to get a son or daughter in drug rehab or being at the graduation from junior college, getting a lawyer or being at the bedside when they stopped life support, the first mass for a new acolyte, going to the police station to protest brutality or blessing a new home—all of these are the stuff of the life of a pastor and I was invited to walk with the people in good times and bad.

One special example of the pastoral presence was with the seniors. I started their club four months after I arrived. The club has been a special treasure for them. There has been a lot of life and a lot of death in these years. The group has two plaques in the parish hall. One has the names of the living members. The other has those who are deceased. I have celebrated the Mass of the Resurrection for over twenty of the group. These funerals have a way of reaching deep down and stirring the waters to surface some of the fundamental issues of life.

One day, after one of these funerals I ran across a book *Here on the Way to There: A Catholic Perspective on Dying and What Follows* [15] that I never would have noticed earlier in my life. It was on aging, dying, and death. The author, William Shannon, a Merton expert, is one of my favorites. I was ready for it. After reading it, I proposed to the seniors that I give a retreat on these topics. They agreed. So I did the retreat and it was on target for the folks. It also started me on a journey.

As so often in my life, I had a clear picture in my mind. The book gave me a dynamic handle on the big trio of aging, dying, and death. I wrote a letter on the theme for the Sunday bulletin. It grabbed the attention of a lot of people. I said we should face the reality of death and make it front and center. To be real about death is to face the very clear fact that death is an essential part of life. It is going to happen, not in general, but to me. To be real about our death does not mean a time of morbidity and despair, walking around as if all is lost. On the contrary, we are called to plunge into life with enthusiasm and joy. We need to live with full attention on the present. Today is God's great gift. We do not know about tomorrow and yesterday is gone.

The Sacrament of the Present Moment

I was gifted to express the issue in a practical and concrete way. The problem for me, however, was the familiar journey. How do I move from the head to the heart? How do I make it real?

God had a plan to help me. God's plan does not guarantee a worry free environment protected by my wise investments. It is a movement to eternal life. God's plan is called aging.

I was shocked when the doctor told me I was on the fast track to diabetes. I needed a huge change in my diet. I began to notice new and slowly increasing difficulty in remembering common words in Spanish. I had always been great with names. Now, it is a real cross to come up blank so often. Then there was the death of a first sibling when my sister Mary died. This was followed by brother, Tim. It appears people never tire of telling me how great I look, but my energy does not seem to flow from the good appearance. In other words, I really am getting older. It was reaching me with a steady diminishment in so many parts of my life. More importantly, I started not only to accept it, but to enter into it as part of God's plan.

Aging finds meaning when we keep our eye on the ball. It does not make it easy but understanding and accepting God's plan makes sense.

Shannon's book on aging laid out a beautiful description of the aging process. It is God's way of drawing us into the mystery of love that is the Father, Son, and Holy Spirit. This is why we were created. This is our goal. Aging is moving us along the path that God has laid out.

My task these last several years has been to try to own this reality in all of its beauty and to move away from the illusion of immortality hidden in my pills, my discipline to regular exercise, and a good diet and the seemingly endless visits to my many doctors. Of course, we need to take care of ourselves and I am really good at it. Yet God is in charge of the clock, and with good purpose. He is bringing us home on his schedule. In the meanwhile, we have today. We need to live it with all the talent, time, and treasure the Lord has given us to use responsibly and with love. My struggle has been to really live out of this clear vision. I have some good days and some days laden with self-deception and denial.

Move to the Carmelite Message

There were two women in the parish that had tragedies in their families that were far beyond horrendous. One was a domestic violence pattern that finally resulted in a beating so bad that one side of the wife's face was crushed and she spent several weeks in a comma. The husband was killed by the police in this culminating incident of many years of violence. The other was a case of indescribable sexual abuse.

One day in 2007, as I watched these two women at prayer, it touched me very deeply. Their prayer seemed special and very deep. I had an idea. I suggested that we read Teresa of Avila's *Interior Castle*. The effort never really got off the ground but it was the seed of a much more fruitful venture.

I began presenting teachings on Carmelite spirituality as part of my weekly Bible classes. This led to a ten week summer class completely on Carmelite spirituality. The people became hungry for more. They were like the disciples with the Lord, "Teach us to pray."

The next development was a retreat for all the Lay Carmelites in the Los Angeles area. I used Jack Welch's book, *Seasons of the Heart: The Spiritual Dynamic of the Carmelite Life*.[16] It proved to be very effective on several levels. First, it presented a summary of the latest developments on Carmelite Spirituality. Second, it was simple and clear, yet inviting into a much deeper journey. Third, it had a series of drawings of the different stages of the heart on the journey inwards. I made enlargements of these beautiful works of art by Sr. Catherine Martin, O. Carm., and placed them around the gym for the retreat. They have become a staple of our work in the parish. I have repeated the presentation on the *Seasons of the Heart* over a dozen times in the last six years.

The basic outline of Jack Welch's book is the five seasons of the heart. The first is the Longing Heart. The universal hunger is for happiness but only God can ultimately satisfy this hunger. Our dilemma is the second season, the Enslaved Heart, where we pursue the false gods of our addictions, attachments, and idols. The third season is the Listening Heart where God enkindles a deeper love to free us from our clinging to all that keeps us from God. The fourth season is the Troubled Heart where God continues the purifying process through the events of life. Finally, the last season is a Pure Heart where God transforms the desires of the heart to direct them into the Mystery of love.

Also at this time, in 2006, another Carmelite friend, Fr. Ernie Larkin, released a book, *Contemplative Prayer for Today: Christian Meditation.*[17] For me, it was one of those "right place, right time and right message" moments. I was ready for it.

The message, like anything that is truly Gospel in its content and spirit, is both simple and profound. There are many riches in the book, but the one that I was ready for was the actual practice of Christian meditation. This involves two periods of silent prayer, in the morning and the evening, of twenty to thirty minutes. These prayer times are like bookends of the day to help us live in the presence of God. The prayer is consciously aimed at being contemplative. The goal is to use a mantra, **Maranatha,** and repeat it steadily to quiet the mind and to aim at a measure of silence for God's language is silence. The prayer does not aim at any feeling of peace. It seeks only to quiet us down to let God work at the depths within us. Its success is measured only by the way we live.

Back at Notre Dame in 1977, I faced the question, "What do you want to be when you grow up?" I responded, "I want to be a Carmelite." I really had a fuzzy idea of what that meant. So did the Carmelite Order in the post Vatican II period when all religious orders were called to return to their sources, to rediscover their charism. It has been a wonderful journey of searching and seeking and finding for the Order and for me personally over these decades.

So as these events of the retreats on the *Season of the Heart* and Ernie's *Christian Meditation* and the beautiful enthusiasm of the people for more Carmelite spirituality evolved, another surprise occurred. The people wanted to focus this journey of almost three years by joining the Lay Carmelites. In the final preparation for that, I spent an entire semester in 2011 of having them pray together on Wednesday evenings. It consisted of a half hour of Christian meditation and a half hour of *lectio divina* with time for reflection and sharing. We jointly moved more deeply and clearly into the Carmelite life. One concrete and beautiful expression of this Carmelite enthusiasm took place on the feast of Our Lady of Mt. Carmel on July 16, 2011. Over forty adult members of the parish made simple vows as Lay Carmelites. Another group will join them in July 2013.

In all of this new Carmelite enthusiasm, I was building on a special experience I had on retreat in 2007. I wrote this on August 1, 2007:

"In June, reading Jack Welch's book, *The Carmelite Way*, had a big impact on me. I received a clear call for a more specifically contemplative lifestyle. The combination of the reflections on the Carmelite tradition and prayer and the regular practice of Christian Meditation have resulted in a clear and definite change in my lifestyle.

Here are some of the changes:

Real reduction of time to TV sports and the huge amount of time I generally waste in this area;

A very big cut back in TV time for almost all other than news;

More spiritual reading and prayer;

A strong call into the Carmelite tradition;

More present to what I am doing and simply more interest in the whole process of ministry and living in community;

In prayer, I have a desire to bring love more into my experience. I pray often for purity of heart;

Keith Egan has a very meaningful quote at the end of his opening chapter of his book on Carmelite prayer, "Carmelite prayer is all about letting God create within one a magnanimous, loving heart;"

…After this retreat with all its avalanche of grace, I need to go back and enter into life. Prayer and recollection and humility are very necessary but life and a hunger to do God's will are the goal. I need to avoid spiritualizing things and be open to the call of justice and commitment to the people and the poor."

When I returned to the flow of events in the parish, I was not surprised that I failed to live up the beautiful reflections of my retreat. I was reminded of my great experience on retreat in 1988. I had this attractive ideal in front of me calling me forth. My response was a fragmented heart that ever so slowly began to make the ideal more real. Here too, almost twenty years later in 2007, the stop and go process continues. The strong pull into the Carmelite tradition and prayer to seek the face of living God has been a magnet pulling me grudgingly and slowly into the future. God must know well if we did not fall on our face fairly regularly we would be impossible to live with.

The Eucharist

Another area of the contemplative pull has been the Eucharist. In recent years, the celebration of the Eucharist in the parish is truly different. It has become steadily a deeper and richer experience for me. One big factor is my journey during these years with the people. I have been there for a lot of life with them.

One of the TV attractions in the Hispanic community is the "telenovela", an adult soap opera that floods the TV screens nightly. I have been blessed to be part of a good many of the people's personal "telenovelas." I tell the people there are a thousand "telenovelas" in each pew.

When I am preaching and when I am celebrating the Eucharist, I look at the congregation with a deep sense of connection.

There is an old saying that a young teacher often teaches what he does not know. A mature teacher teaches only what he does know. A wise teacher teaches only what is necessary. I think this applies to preachers also.

In my preaching, I have slowly moved closer to being the wise preacher. I have tried to focus simply on a few points that are always part of my homily. God's love for us is without limits and without conditions. I conclude my reflection in a way to lead into a point I constantly repeat. We need to walk with Jesus.

The homily is always wrapped up in these points: God's love calls us to walk with Jesus. The details from the day's Scriptures simply make concrete the recurring message: walking in love with Jesus.

In the celebration of the Eucharistic prayer, I look out at the congregation and have a real sense of the Body of Christ, here and now. It is a privileged moment for me and becoming more so with the passage of time. It is one clear moment when the journey from the head to heart is most complete and a moment of the truly real.

Mother Teresa Calls

In 2007, I felt a call to read and study St. Teresa of Avila. It seemed to connect to my desire to embrace a contemplative lifestyle. I liked her hardnosed practicality and her down to earth simplicity. Her emphasis on knowing ourselves was becoming front and center in my journey. Most of all, I truly loved her statement that, in the end, all of our lives are the story of God's mercy. So I was ready to rediscover Mother Teresa.

I developed a workshop for the parish on her *Interior Castle*. I repeated the workshop a few times in the parish and once again, I invited the Lay Carmelites in Los Angeles to join us for a day with Mother Teresa. Then I had a new idea.

When I go to Chicago, I stay with my sister Therese who continues to run the home for women in recovery called St. Martin de Porres House of Hope. I suggested to Therese that my workshop on the *Interior Castle* would be good for the women. She was thrilled at the prospect. Teresa's theme of self-knowledge was right on target for the women. Teresa wrote, quoting her experience of Jesus, "When you find yourself, you will find me." This really made sense with the women because this project of self-knowledge was their full time job in recovery. They had all kinds of group experiences, Narcotics Anonymous meetings, Alcoholics Anonymous meetings, and personal counseling along with communal living. What lit a fire in their hearts was Teresa's message that we are the Interior Castle, and that the interior journey ultimately leads to God. God is the final destiny of our self-knowledge. This was a forceful connection to spirituality that few were able to name but most were beginning to experience in their recovery. They knew they needed God. They knew, in a new and different way, they wanted God.

Many of the women are poor. Most are African American and many are not well educated. All are recovering drug addicts. They got the message. One spoke for the group when she said, "Teresa has better stuff from four hundred years ago than I have in my anger management class today."

St. Teresa is no longer a visitor at the St. Martin's. She has taken up residence.

Since then, I have done three more presentations to the women on Teresa and Carmelite spirituality.

Moving from "Been There All Along"

All of these experiences of aging, moving to the Carmelite message, the new, deeper and expanded presence at the Eucharist, and the arrival of St. Teresa were expressions of a new dimension in my life. I was aware of God's presence in a new way.

Much more often, it was no longer a blazing insight from a distance that "God had been there all along." Now, in some vague, but very real way it was "God is here all along." This is the contemplative switch.

Conclusion

One of the things that is clear about life is that far too often we do not get a second chance. That means we have to live with the consequences of our mistakes and, hopefully, learn from them. Looking back over the decades, I can see clearly how I was too prone to create "either/or" choices for myself. I say frequently now that there are not two sides to every story. There usually are nine or ten sides if we dig deep enough.

My journey as a Catholic, a priest, and a Carmelite had both benefited and suffered from the historic changes in society and the post Vatican II world. In the midst of these truly tumultuous times, I was blessed and challenged to participate in two of the great migrations of our time, and according to some experts, of all time: the movement of the African Americans from the South to the North in the post World War II era and the migration of the Hispanics from Latin America to the Unites States in the last several decades.

I was on the front lines. I had to make decisions that were immediate, concrete, and real. More often than I like to admit, the decisions were lacking in depth of personal integrity and intellectual discipline.

It seems to me my entire journey to discover this personal authenticity in my Carmelite heritage was gifted because I stayed in the struggle. I slowly grew in humility and I was able to admit limits, confusion, and the illusions that hid self interest.

This is why Woody Allen's quaint saying that life is 95 percent a matter of just showing up is real for me. Teresa of Avila's saying that the story of our lives is the story of God's mercy just becomes clearer by the day.

In 2004 in a letter to the Carmelite family, Fr. Joseph Chalmers, the prior general of the Order at the time, wrote the following passage. I believe it is an expression of the growth of Carmelite self-understanding in the years after Vatican II that has been so fundamental to my journey.

> "Our vocation as Carmelites is very profound. We are called to serve the people as contemplative communities. By responding to Christ's call to follow him, we pledge ourselves to take on his vision and values but we soon find that we are incapable of living up to our own ideals on our own. As we mature in our relationship with God, we give space to God to purify us so that we begin to see the way God sees and love as God loves. This way of seeing and loving is painful for the human being because it requires a radical transformation of heart." [18]

I am grateful to share my story for those in my era so that it may help you to understand so much of the times we have shared in common. I hope my story will help for those in their middle years to see the light in their confusion. Finally, for the young people I hope I can give hope to remain faithful and searching for the God who is there all the time.

Endnotes

1. James McClendon, *Biography as Theology: How Life Stories Can Remake Today's Theology* (Philadelphia, PA: Trinity Press International, 1990), p. viii.

2. John Welch, O. Carm., *The Carmelite Way: An Ancient Path for Today's Pilgrim* (Mahwah, New Jersey: Paulist Press, 1996) pp. 23-24.

3. These are titles of Academy Award winning movies in 1944 and 1955. They portray a priest who was a cultural breakthrough for the time. In the first, *Going My Way*, Bing Crosby is a warm, human priest deeply involved in the concrete realities of the people especially the youth.

   In *On the Waterfront* Karl Madden goes beyond the ordinary and gets involved in confronting the unjust treatment of the dock workers by the corrupt union under control of the mob.

4. After a few years Fr. Edward Egan returned to Rome to teach. Three decades later he returned to the US and was soon the Cardinal Archbishop of New York. In the second Eucharistic Prayer for children there is a phrase I love. It says we should pray for those we do not love as we should. Cardinal Egan receives my prayers often.

5. The Woodlawn Organization was a local community organization that was started by Saul Alinsky in 1960. It was nationally famous at the time in the 1960s.

6. *Chicago Defender*, March 15, 1969, p. 2.

7. *Chicago Daily News*, October 12, 1971, p. 1).

8. Gregory Baum, *Man Becoming: God in Secular Experience* (New York, New York: Herder and Herder New York, 1970).

9. Pope John XXXIII, Pacem in Terris, #112.

10. Dwight D. Eisenhower, *Address to the American Society of Newspaper Editors*, Washington, DC., April 16, 1953.

11. John Welch, O. Carm., *Spiritual Pilgrims: Carl Jung and Teresa of Avila* (Mahwah, New Jersey: Paulist Press, 1982).

12. Gerald May, *Addiction and Grace* (Harper Collier Publishers, San Francisco, CA, 1988).

13. Mesters emphasized the three ways of strife through which the prophet Elijah tried to re-establish justice in Israel.

   The walk of justice: i.e. against the false ideologies of his time and toward a concrete experience of the need for Yahweh, the God of his people.

   The walk of solidarity: Elijah examines and takes within his embrace the victims of injustice. The alliance with God is needed to combat the disgrace of poverty and to make it possible for all to participate in the goods which God has given all.

   The walk of the mystic: Elijah strove to restore the self-confidence of the poor by a renewal of the consciences of all by the words uttered to both the poor and oppressed that God is with them.

   These three walks must be integrated or they become distorted:

   Justice of itself without solidarity and the mystic "walk" ends in political action without humanity and without plumbing of the depths of the human spirit.

   Solidarity alone becomes pure philanthropy which deceives the conscience and mutes the cry of the poor.

   The mystic "**walk**" without justice and solidarity becomes an alienated piety which is not found in reality nor in the life of our Father Elijah and even offends God and the poor. (Carmelite General Chapter, Chapter Documents and Decrees: Rome, 1983, p. 13).

14.   James H. Forest, "Merton's Peacemaking," *Sojourners*. December 1979, p.18. Forest quotes a personal letter received from Merton.

15.   William H. Shannon, *Here on the Way to There: A Catholic Perspective on Dying and What Follows* (Cincinnati, Ohio: St. Anthony Messenger Press, 1989).

16.   John Welch, O. Carm., *Seasons of the Heart: The Spiritual Dynamic of the Carmelite Life* (Darien, IL: Carmelite Media, 2008).

17.   Ernest Larkin, O. Carm., *Contemplative Prayer for Today: Christian Meditation* (Singapore: Medio Media, 2007).

18.   Joseph Chalmers, O. Carm., *The God of Our Contemplation: A Letter of the Prior General to the Carmelite Family* (Rome: General Curia of the Carmelite Order, January 1, 2004).

CPSIA information can be obtained at www.ICGtesting.com
Printed in the USA
LVOW07s1441141213

365310LV00003B/7/P